Great Photoshop Techniques

Tim Meehan

MIS:
PRESS

A Subsidiary of
Henry Holt and Co., Inc.

MIS:Press
A Subsidiary of Henry Holt and Company, Inc.
115 West 18th Street
New York, New York 10011

Library of Congress Cataloging-in-Publication Data

Meehan, Tim, 1959–
    Great Photoshop techniques / Tim Meehan.
        p. cm.
      ISBN 1-55828-366-8 : $39.95

    1. Computer graphics. 2. Adobe Photoshop.   I. Title.
T385.M425   1994
006.6'869--dc20   94-21065
                                                       CIP

97   96   95   94   4 3 2 1

Publisher: Brenda McLaughlin

Development Editor: Michael Sprague

Technical Editor/Production Editor: Eileen Mullin

Associate Production Editor: Cari Geffner

Copy Editor: Jo Ann Arnott

Table of Contents

1 Wood Textures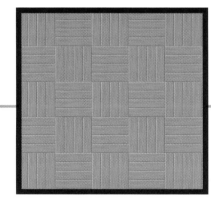...............page 1

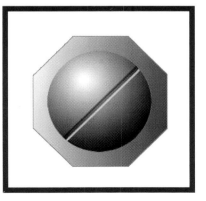

2 Metallic Textures..............page 29

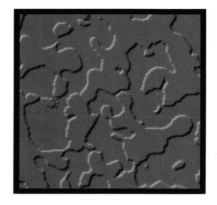

3 Creating Rocks and Gravels...............page 51

4 Tiles and Bricks..............page 73

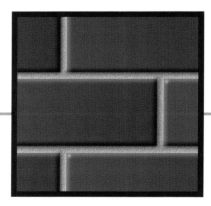

5 Creating Environments..............page 99

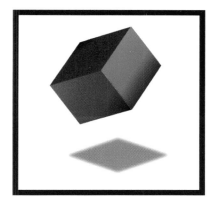

6 Creating 3-D Objects with Photoshop............page 129

7 Creating Special Effects.............page 153

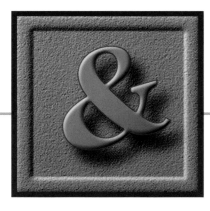

8 Artist's Gallery.............page 185

Acknowledgments

No acknowledgments for a book of this nature would be complete without recognizing the creators of the enabling technology. To all the engineers and technicians at Apple Computer, Inc. and Adobe Systems, Inc.: Thanks Apple! Thanks Adobe! Great products like these help artists everywhere create great work.

Thanks to all the artists and creative professionals everywhere who contributed their expertise and samples of their work to make this a better book and who help make products like Photoshop a popular standard from which we all benefit.

A very special thanks to Susanna Hollenback French for dutifully and cheerfully proofing and play-testing my original material through all the preliminary work and revisions. There's nothing like the affections of a beautiful woman and the pressure of an impending mortgage payment to inspire a man to work late into the night.

Thanks also to my clients, friends, and family (including my spotted dog Ray). You indulged me my lack of time and attention while putting in all the long hours and late nights on this effort to marry words and pictures in a readable format.

Thanks also to the RMHGA and the "Front Range Boys" paragliding pilots for joining me in a consuming pastime that afforded a welcome distraction and consistent inspiration that never failed to fuel my creativity.

Introduction

Welcome to the exciting world of Adobe Photoshop! You are about to embark on a marvelous adventure of discovery. In this book you will find new and easy ways to create all kinds of fantastic visual effects and textures with your computer and Photoshop. All the techniques are presented in an easy to follow step-by-step format. You don't have to be an expert computer or Photoshop user to get the most out of this book.

Why Should You Use this Book?

If you are a beginner with Adobe Photoshop, a seasoned professional, or anyone in-between, you will find this book of great value. It shows you many different techniques and how to create a wonderful variety of textures that you can use in almost any application.

You will find uses for the techniques as colorful and textural backgrounds and illustrative ornaments in:

- Multimedia presentations and slide shows
- Desktop publishing, graphic design, and printing applications
- Software and application environment development
- Professional digital illustrations and image retouching

If, for nothing else, Adobe Photoshop is the ultimate painting and retouching tool, allowing the casual user as well as the serious professional a wonderful tool for artistic expression.

Understanding the Techniques

Just as there is more than one way to skin the proverbial cat, there are probably several ways to accomplish each of the effects shown in this book. The idea is to provide the simplest, most direct method, with a minimum of complexity and calculation. The intention is to create a friendly, inviting, "workshop" learning environment that will help you create stunning visual effects quickly and easily without causing your brain to implode from keeping track of countless layers and channels.

It is important to note that the techniques and effects presented in this book are by no means the ultimate this-is-the-one-and-only-best-way-to-do-this methods. Every effort has been made to present a simple, step-by-step format for creating some effective and, most importantly, useful Photoshop projects so that you can learn the best features and effects this program has to offer.

Some Hints and Tips

Don't be afraid to experiment with any of the techniques presented. All the examples are intended to be fundamental starting points onto which you can build your own personal collection of special tricks and techniques. Chances are, as you're working through the demonstrations, you will think of ways to enhance the technique to fit a special need of your own.

Often, subtle changes in the filter parameter settings can create completely new and different visual effects from what you see in the demonstration figures. You may want to write a note or two to accompany your document, describing the changes you made in the filters to achieve the effects. You can enter notes in the Comments area of the Info window (Document Info dialog box), which you can access from the desktop by choosing the document and then, from the File menu, choosing Get Info. Another way is to create a simple text file using any word processor or the TeachText utility that came with your Macintosh.

Create a new folder for your work as you create new images using the techniques shown here. As you progress through the examples, you will begin to amass quite a collection of new textures and techniques that you will want to save and reuse in your future Photoshop documents. In fact, you may want to create a few different folders to store your new work, separating them by type (techniques, textures, patterns, and so forth). You can also store any notes you have taken while creating these documents.

Image File Formats

With so many choices for image file formats, how do you know which format is best? The following table lists the Photoshop image file formats.

If your use is	Then save your file as
Art for printing in color (CMYK)	CMYK TIFF
Black and white line art	Bitmapped PICT
Grayscale halftones for printing	Grayscale TIFF
Color multimedia applications	32-bit color PICT
Import into PostScript drawing programs	32-bit EPS
Export into DOS or Windows	BMP or PCX (remember to include a ".BMP" or ".PCX" extension on the file name

The Right Tool for the Job

What are the computer requirements to make the most of this book? Almost any Macintosh computer will get the job done, although the speed depends on the processor, memory, and a few other pertinent details. Adobe Photoshop runs on any of the newer Macintosh computers with at least 4 megabytes of RAM.

Generally, a good rule of thumb is more and faster are better. The more RAM you have in your machine, the faster the processor; the more space you have available on your hard disk drive, the more work you will be able to get done with Photoshop. And, the larger and denser your images are, the longer your work will take to complete.

Following are the hardware requirements for working efficiently with Photoshop:

- You should have a 68020 or better CPU. The faster processors in the 68040 (or in the PowerPC) CPU families give a noticeable and significant improvement in your wait time while Photoshop processes images. The most potent demonstration of this effect is to actually watch Photoshop running on two different classes of computers side by side.

Remember, time is cumulative. The few extra seconds it takes a slower machine to work for you add up over the course of a week, robbing you of time. While you're working late on Friday evening, someone else on a faster machine is already home eating dinner and thinking about a restful weekend.

- Plenty of RAM memory. System 7.1 and subsequent Macintosh operating systems will gobble up about 4 megabytes of RAM. Adobe recommends 3 to 5 megabytes of RAM. In the case of RAM, Photoshop has its own scheme for creating virtual RAM by using available hard disk space. This means that when you have reached the limits of the available RAM memory in your system, Photoshop will start using hard disk space for RAM. When this happens, program operation will slow down considerably.

- A full-color monitor. A monitor capable of displaying all 16.7 million colors (or 24 bits of the recorded data) is your best bet. Photoshop works just fine with less capable monitors, but the images you see on your screen will be different than what is actually being manipulated by the program. Once again, the best demonstration of this difference is to see 8-bit color images next to 24-bit color images.

If you own an older Macintosh with a slower processor, there are third-party options available to you to accelerate your CPU. Generally these solutions are a good substitute for buying a brand new, faster machine, although it's a good idea to shop around your local computer reseller. You will be surprised at how little the new machines are selling for.

In the case of RAM, hard disk space, and processing speed: like so many other things in life, more is better and too much is never enough.

Chapter 1

Wood Textures

This chapter explains how to create wood textures to use as backgrounds or as textural detail. They're simple to create and can be infinitely customized to fit almost any application.

In this chapter, you begin by creating a simple wood grain design that you color in different ways to look like various types of wood. Then you learn how to create different wood patterns to simulate wood paneling and woven woods.

This technique is a simple but powerful effect that can be used in the background as a generic wood wall or floor texture, or in the foreground as textural detail for objects, signs, or special lettering effects.

Throughout this and other technique demonstrations, remember to save your work often. You can save it into a library file of textures that you can draw from and apply as often as you like. All the techniques are simple to produce, require no scanning, and can be easily customized and created at any resolution.

Creating a Simple Wood Texture

Let's start by creating a simple wood pattern. This effect is a useful tool for creating warm, home-like environments in your renderings. It makes a great background or accent texture. You will see how a few simple color variations can change the character of the texture, creating the look of different types of wood. You can use this texture as a floor, a wall, or as wood accents for baseboards, picture frames, or even simple objects like furniture.

The steps that you follow to begin this effect are the same steps that you will use to create most of the textures in this chapter. As you progress, note how some of the basic techniques are repeated for each new effect.

To create a wood texture, follow these steps:

Step 1.

Choose **New** from the **File** menu to create a new document.

Step 2.

Enter 640 pixels for the width and 480 pixels for the height. Enter 72 pixels/inch for the resolution. Click the Mode pop-up menu and choose RGB Color.

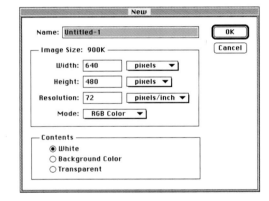

Step 3.

Double-click the Rectangular Marquee tool from the toolbar to assign a defined selection area. Set the options to select a single column of pixels.

Step 4.

Click the top left corner of your working area. This will automatically select a single column of pixels along the left edge of your image.

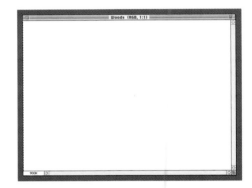

Step 5.

Add gaussian noise to the column of pixels by choosing **Add Noise** from the **Noise** submenu of the **Filter** menu. Set the amount to 999.

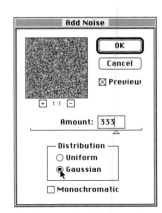

Step 6.

Choose **Scale** from the **Effects** submenu of the **Image** menu. Using the mouse, drag the bottom right scale handle all the way to the right to stretch your selection all the way across your image.

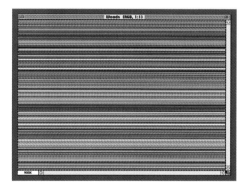

Step 7.

For a more lifelike effect, you need to blur the selection. Choose **Blur More** from the **Blur** submenu of the **Filter** menu. This softens the streaks a bit.

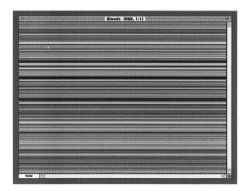

This is a good start, but it hardly has a woody look to it. Next, you need to add some color to the wood texture. Follow these steps:

Step 1.

Choose **Hue/Saturation** from the **Adjust** submenu of the **Image** menu (the keyboard shortcut is Command-U). Make sure that you check the Colorize and Preview check box options in the Hue/Saturation dialog box so you can view your changes.

Step 2.

Drag the Hue slider to the right a bit (or type 30 in the value field) to change the color range of the selection to a warm, oak tone.

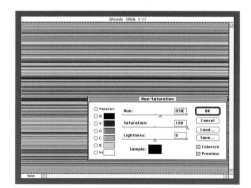

Step 3.

Click OK.

In the next operation, you change the texture, so you should save the existing document and edit a copy of it. To create an exact copy of the coarse wood grain texture, choose **Duplicate** from the **Calculate** submenu of the **Image** menu.

Now the texture is getting pretty close. The color range is pretty natural, but the streaks (or grain) are still coarse. To compress the streaks to something that's a bit more natural looking, follow these steps:

Step 1.

Choose **All** from the **Select** menu to select the entire image.

Step 2.

Choose **Scale** from the **Effects** submenu of the **Image** menu.

Step 3.

Drag the top right corner handle straight down. This compresses the pixels vertically to give you a more natural wood-like effect.

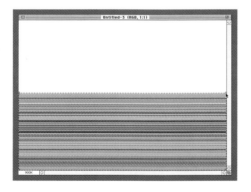

Step 4.

Finally, choose **Crop** from the **Edit** menu to exclude all the unselected areas in your image.

Not bad for a first effort!

Changing the Color

You can play with the color mixtures to change the character of the wood. The simplest way to adjust the color intensity of the texture is to change its brightness and contrast.

Choose **Brightness/Contrast** from the Adjust submenu of the **Image** menu. Try a few variations. Change the brightness to 30 and the contrast value to -30.

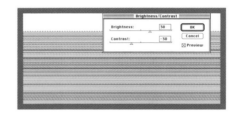

Try changing the brightness value to 60 and the contrast value to -60.

This flattens out the color range and gives you a little more of a blond look. Save this selection in your work folder as Blonde.

Similarly, you can also darken the texture by setting the brightness to -60 and the contrast to 0. This gives a medium Maple or Walnut tone to your wood grain.

When you create something you like, save it by choosing **Save As** from the **File** menu.

Changing the Grain

How about adding a little of nature's randomness to your wood grain? You can curve the grain a little bit to give it more life. Follow these steps:

Step 1.

Open your coarse wood grain texture and choose **All** from the **Select** menu.

Step 2.

Choose **Wave** from the **Distort** submenu of the **Filter** menu.

Step 3.

Change the settings in the Wave dialog box to those shown below. Make sure you click the Wrap Around radio button.

Number of generators	18
Wavelength	Min31/Max900
Amplitude	2/30
Horizontal	50%
Vertical	100%

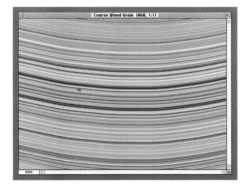

You can also try a few different variations of these settings to exaggerate the effect.

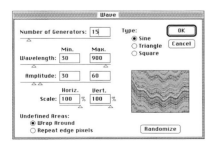

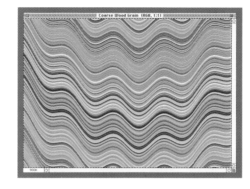

Step 4.

Apply the same filter again (use keyboard shortcut Command-F to repeat any filter) and see how your image can become even more randomly gnarled.

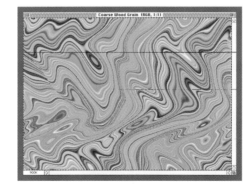

Choose **Save As** from the **File** menu as often as you like to save your variations with their great colors and textures. You will create an impressive library of textures before your work with this book finished.

Creating a Rough Wood Texture

This section discusses another way to simulate a wooden texture with Photoshop. This technique gives you the same color control over your wood texture, but applies a slightly different and rougher looking texture that can be customized to simulate antique woods, aging barn woods, or rough wicker textures. It's a simple enhancement to the basic wood texture you just learned that uses the colorizing feature under the Image menu.

Follow these steps:

Step 1.

Start by creating a new document measuring 640 by 480 pixels in RGB Color mode with a resolution of 72 pixels/inch.

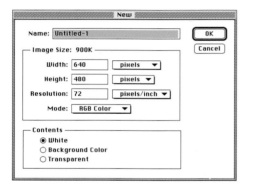

Step 2.

Choose **All** from the **Select** menu to select the entire working area.

Step 3.

Apply a random video noise pattern to the selection by choosing **Add Noise** from the **Noise** submenu of the **Filter** menu. Set the amount to 999 to fill the area with a dense scattering of pixels.

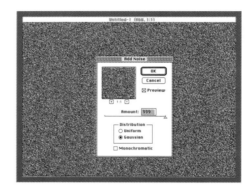

Step 4.

Choose **Motion Blur** from the **Blur** submenu of the **Filter** menu. Set the angle to 0° to keep the stretch horizontal and set the distance to 60 pixels.

Step 5.

Repeat the same filter (by pressing Command-F) to smooth out the stretched pixels laterally.

Step 6.

Choose **Hue/ Saturation** from the **Adjust** submenu of the **Image** menu (or press Command-U).

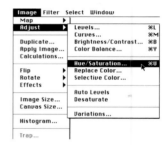

Step 7.

Click the Colorize and Preview check boxes. Then, to create a rich chocolate brown wood texture, set the values to Hue: 30, Saturation: 60, and Lightness: -30. Click OK.

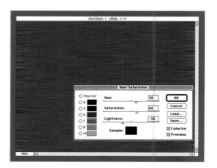

Step 8.

To add a rough weathered texture to your wood, choose **Sharpen More** from the **Sharpen** submenu of the **Filter** menu.

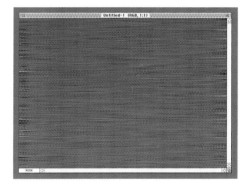

The Sharpen command looks for contrasting color pixels in the selected area and enhances that contrast to create harder edges between color transitions.

Can you see the difference?

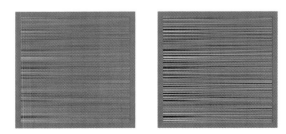

Step 9.

Try changing the color range by entering different values in the **Brightness/Contrast** dialog box.

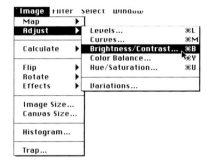

You can achieve some interesting effects by moving the **Brightness/Contrast** sliders back and forth.

Save each of these iterations of the rougher wood concept as background textures in your library of images. Then, after you have created an impressive library of woods to draw on, you can move on to the next section, which discusses creating patterns with these textures.

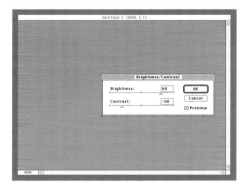

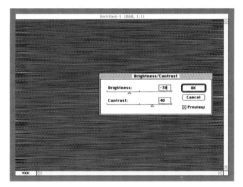

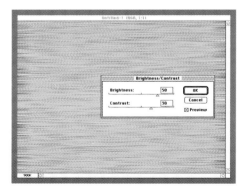

Woven Wood Textures

This section discusses a simple application of Photoshop's capability to use objects as pattern tiles to fill a selected area. This exercise is a good introduction to creating patterns in Photoshop.

Remember, you can customize this effect to fit different applications. It's easy to create your pattern tiles at any proportion, making a broad picnic basket texture as easy to create as an intricate wicker weave texture.

In this exercise, you use a simple technique to simulate the woven woods in some baskets and panels. It involves most of the same steps that you have already been through, with a new mathematical twist. (Yikes! Math? Not to worry.) As with most of the techniques shown in this book, the software does all the work.

Follow these steps:

Step 1.

Create a new document as before, measuring 640 by 480 pixels and in RGB Color mode with a resolution of 72 pixels/inch.

Step 2.

Select an area in your image that is roughly 300 pixels wide by 50 pixels tall. To do this, first choose **Show Info** from the **Windows** menu. Then click the Rectangular Marquee tool and drag over the image; the Info palette will display the height (H) and width (W) of the marquee as you drag. You also can double-click the Rectangular Marquee tool in the tool palette and enter a fixed size of 300 by 50 pixels.

Step 3.

Choose **Add Noise** from the **Noise** submenu of the **Filter** menu. Set the amount to 333 and select Gaussian distribution.

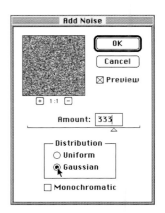

Step 4.

Stretch the noisy pixels by choosing **Motion Blur** from the **Blur** submenu of the **Filter** menu. Set the distance to 120 pixels.

Step 5.

Choose **Sharpen More** from the **Sharpen** submenu of the **Filter** menu to add a little textural contrast to the selection.

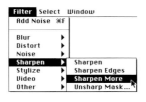

Step 6.

Next, you need to choose the type and age of the woven wood. Choose **Hue/Saturation** from the **Adjust** submenu of the **Image** menu.

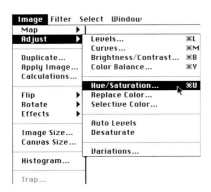

Make sure that the Colorize and Preview check boxes are clicked. Move the sliders for Hue, Saturation, and Brightness until you achieve your favorite wood color.

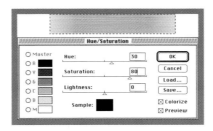

Step 7.

To turn this simple wood section into a woven pattern, you need to make a copy of the selection to paste in as another part of the pattern. Choose **Copy** from the **Edit** menu to place a copy of the current selection onto the clipboard.

It would be pretty easy to define this simple shape as a pattern as is. Choose **Define Pattern** from the **Edit** menu. The selection deselects itself.

Choose **All** from the **Select** menu.

Choose **Fill** from the **Edit** menu.

Choose Pattern and 100% opacity to fill the area with the new pattern.

This isn't quite what you wanted. It is a repeating pattern that appears too regular. Later in the chapter, you will use a similar technique to create a wood paneling effect. But, to create a woven wood effect, you have to stagger the pattern. So, while the area is still selected, press the Delete key to delete the selection. Choose **Paste** from the **Edit** menu or use the keyboard shortcut Command-V to paste the original wood strip back into the picture.

Now to create a staggered pattern. You need two halves of a pattern tile to appear below the original pattern tile. In order for a staggered pattern to match up seamlessly, the two halves must be of equal length and exactly half of their original width. Let's let the machine do the math for us.

If your Info palette is still visible, you will see the exact width (in pixels) of the current selection. You need to use the Rectangular Marquee tool to create a measuring tool to use as a guide for your next pattern tile. Follow these steps:

Step 1.

Double-click the Rectangular Marquee tool. Click the Fixed Size radio button and set the width of the selection to one-half of the original width (150) and the height to 3 pixels.

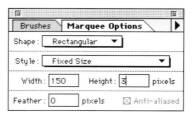

Step 2.

Choose **None** from the **Select** menu (or press Command-D).

Step 3.

You may want to enlarge your view by using the Magnifying tool to click once on the corner of your wood strip (or you can use the keyboard shortcut Command-+).

Step 4.

Choose the Rectangular Marquee tool and click once near the bottom left corner of your image. Your new rectangular selection should be aligned vertically with the left-most pixel of the image.

If it isn't aligned properly, just click again until the selection is lined up correctly. Each time you click with the

Rectangular Marquee tool, you will create a new selection with the same dimensions.

Step 5.

Next, you need to fill your foreground with a color. Choose **Fill** from the **Edit** menu. It doesn't matter what color your foreground is right now, as long as it is not white. Make sure that you choose Foreground from the pop-up menu.

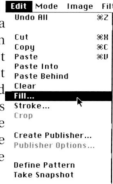

Step 6.

Choose OK to fill the area.

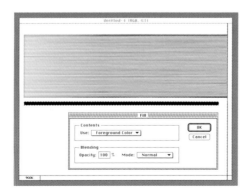

There, that's done. You have just created a marker to show where to position your next pattern tiles. Now for the final piece of the puzzle.

Step 7.

Choose **Paste** from the **Edit** menu (the keyboard shortcut is Command-V). Position the new selection near the place marker you just created.

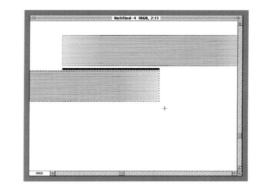

Step 8.

While you are moving the selection into position, you may want to hide the "marching ants" that surround the selection. You can do this by choosing **Hide Edges** from the **Select** menu (or by pressing Command-H).

Step 9.

Move the selection into position by using the cursor keys to nudge the selection one pixel at a time.

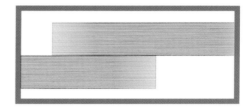

Step 10.

Now you need to finish the pattern tile by creating a new clone of your tile element. Make sure that the Rectangular Marquee tool is still selected. Hold down the Option key, click and hold down the mouse button on our latest wood chip, and then hold down the Shift key and drag the selection straight left until the left edge of the new selection is aligned exactly with the right edge of its clone.

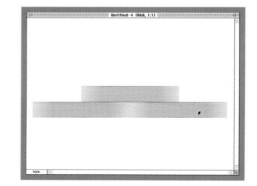

You may find it easier to create the cloned selection and then reposition it using the cursor keys.

Now for the actual pattern definition. You need to select the entire top wood strip and the center halves of the two half-strips underneath. Let the software do the work for you. Remember how you originally set the selection size for the original area to 300 pixels wide by 50 pixels tall? The new selection will be the same width but twice the height. Follow these steps:

Step 1.

Double-click the Rectangular Marquee tool and define the selection area as 300 pixels wide and 100 pixels tall.

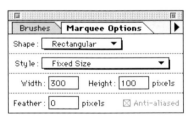

Step 2.

Click the top left corner of the upper wood strip to select the top piece and the two perfectly positioned bottom pieces to create a staggered pattern tile that will match up perfectly when you define it as a pattern.

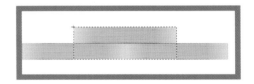

Step 3.

Just for safekeeping, choose **Copy** from the **Edit** menu (you can also press Command-C, or press F3 on an extended keyboard) to preserve a copy of the selection on the clipboard.

Step 4.

Choose **Define Pattern** from the **Edit** menu.

Step 5.

Now, to see the fruits of your labors. Choose **All** from the **Select** menu to select the entire image area.

Step 6.

Choose **Fill** from the **Edit** menu. Make sure that Pattern is selected from the pull-down menu.

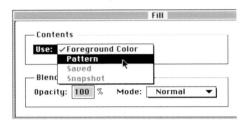

Step 7.

Click OK to fill the selected area with the new pattern.

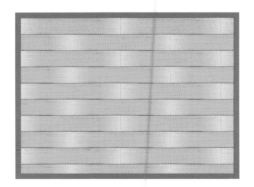

Wow! Check out the woven wood in this image! Don't forget to save this image for use in your personal library of textures.

Creating Wood Paneling

Time to bring the pattern concept together. In this section, you use the wood grain textures to make a pattern of wood panels. Two separate techniques are discussed for simulating tongue-in-groove wood planking and wood paneling.

Creating paneling is a bit more complex than creating a simple repeating pattern. It requires that you to do a little calculating to create a smoothly repeating interleaved pattern, but the results are dramatic and, once created, can be saved and reused often.

To create a new wood plank using some of the techniques you learned in the previous sections, follow these steps:

Step 1.

Start a new document measuring 640 by 480 pixels in RGB Color mode with a resolution of 72 pixels/inch.

Step 2.

Use the Rectangular Marquee tool to create a fairly large area to start your texture.

Step 3.

Fill the area with random video noise by choosing **Add Noise** from the **Noise** submenu of the **Filter** menu. Set the amount to 999 for maximum effect.

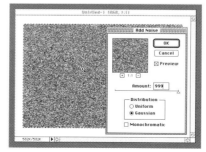

Step 4.

Choose **Motion Blur** from the **Blur** submenu of the **Filter** menu. Set the distance to 120 pixels. This stretches and blurs the pixels across the selection, creating multi-colored streaks.

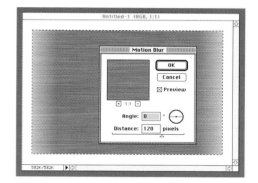

Step 5.

Color the selection by choosing **Hue/Saturation** from the **Adjust** submenu of the **Image** menu (the keyboard shortcut is Command-U). Make sure that the Preview and Colorize check boxes are selected. Set the Hue to 30, the Saturation to 60, and the Lightness to 0. Click OK.

Step 6.

Sharpen the texture just a bit. Choose **Sharpen Move** from the **Sharpen** submenu of the **Filter** menu.

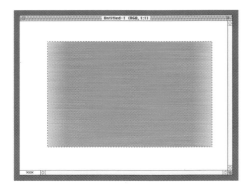

Remember, you can reapply the same filter just by using the keyboard shortcut Command-F. It's easy to adjust the wood grain texture in small increments using this technique. Press Command-F until you get the results you like.

You now have a perfectly acceptable area from which you can select a great-looking strip to use as your first wood plank. Continue with the following steps:

Step 1.

Double-click the Rectangular Marquee tool and assign a defined selection area.

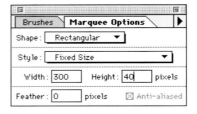

For this demonstration, use a relatively long and narrow area for your selection. Set the horizontal dimension to 300 pixels and the vertical dimension to 40 pixels.

Step 2.

Select an area to use as a wood plank by clicking inside of the newly created wood texture.

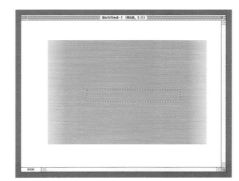

Notice how the Rectangular Marquee selection automatically proportions itself to the exact dimensions you just defined.

Wherever you click, the Rectangular Marquee tool selects an area of exact dimensions using the click point as the top left corner of the area.

If you don't care for the original selection, try clicking on a new area. The texture you see in the selection area will be the texture in each plank you create. Constraining the selection area guarantees that each click selects an area with the exact same size and proportion. Continue clicking until you select an area that looks right for you.

Step 3.

Choose **Inverse** from the **Select** menu to select everything on the page except the selection.

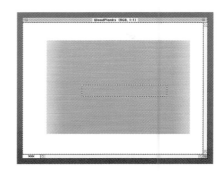

Step 4.

Press the Delete key.

Step 5.

Choose **Inverse** from the **Select** menu again to reselect the plank.

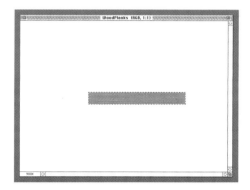

Now let's add some dimension to the plank using a simple channel technique.

Step 1.

Choose **Show Channels** from the **Window** menu.

Step 2.

Click the arrow in the top right corner of the Show Channels palette. A pop-up menu appears.

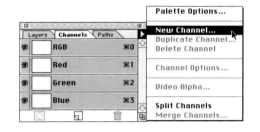

Step 3.

Choose **New Channel** from this menu. Name the channel anything you like.

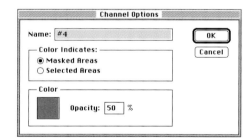

Step 4.

Fill the selection with the black foreground color; this will create a shape that you can select in the new channel. Hold down the Option and Command keys, and then press the Left Arrow key twice and the Up Arrow key twice.

Step 5.

In the Channels palette, click the RGB channel selection. The selection moves two pixels to the left and up.

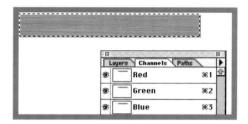

Step 6.

Next, choose the Magic Wand tool.

Step 7.

Hold down the Shift key while you click anywhere in the background. This adds the entire background to the current selection.

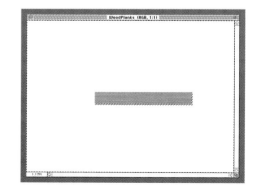

Here's a fun part. You're going to add a shadow edge to this plank to increase its dimensionality. Follow these steps (to see the results of this adjustment as you create the effect, choose **Hide Edges** from the **Select** menu):

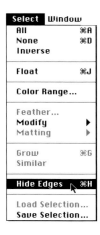

Step 1.

Choose **Inverse** from the **Select** menu to select the remaining pixels along the bottom and right side of the plank.

Step 2.

Choose **Brightness/Contrast** from the **Adjust** submenu of the **Image** menu (or press Command-B).

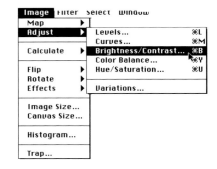

Step 3.

Move the sliders to decrease the brightness just a bit.

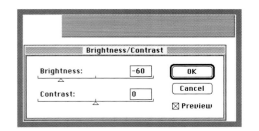

This creates a subtler, darker edge to the plank, simulating three dimensions.

Next, we'll select the top left edge of our plank by moving the plank two pixels in the opposite direction as you did in the previous steps. Follow these steps:

Step 1.

Re-activate channel four to show your black channel shape.

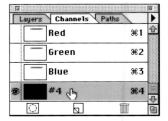

Step 2.

Use the Magic Wand tool to select the plank shape again.

Step 3.

Hold down the Option and Command Keys while you press the Down Arrow key twice and the Right Arrow key twice.

Click again on the RGB channel in the Channels palette.

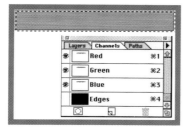

See how only the selection has shifted two pixels over and down?

Now to add a highlight along the top and left edges of the plank. Follow these steps:

Step 1.

First you must select only those pixels along the top and left edges of the plank. Switch back to the fourth channel. Select the Magic Wand tool, hold down the Shift key, and click once in the background area of the image. This adds the entire background to the selection.

Step 2.

Choose **Inverse** from the **Select** menu to select only the top left edges of the plank. Now return to the RGB channel and see how only the top left edge of your plank is selected.

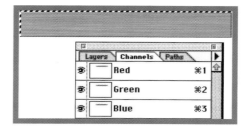

Step 3.

Choose **Hide Edges** from the **Select** menu so that you can see exactly what you're doing.

Step 4.

Choose **Brightness/Contrast** from the **Adjust** submenu of the **Image** menu (or press Command-B).

Step 5.

Move the brightness slider to lighten the selection. See how the process you just completed adds a subtle sense of dimension to the object?

Step 6.

Deselect the area by choosing **None** from the **Select** menu (or press Command-D).

You may want to save this plank illustration as a document to use in other patterned illustrations. Follow these steps:

Step 1.

Choose the Rectangular Marquee tool and click once on the top left corner of the plank. Remember, this tool is still set to select a defined area. In fact, it's set to the very same dimensions as the plank you have just created.

Step 2.

Choose **Copy** from the **Edit** menu (or press Command-C), and then choose **New** from the **File** menu (or press Command-N).

Step 3.

Choose **Paste** from the **Edit** menu (or press Command-V).

Step 4.

Choose **Save** from the **File** menu to save this new document in the working folder for later use as a pattern element.

Now back to the working document. Let's complete the pattern. This pattern will be just a little more complex than the one you created for the woven wood effect. You stagger the pattern in three pieces instead of two. Your wood plank should still be on the clipboard. If it isn't, select it and choose **Copy** from the **Edit** menu (or press Command-C). Follow these steps:

Step 1.

You need to define an area that is one-third as wide as the current wood plank selection. Double-click the Rectangular Marquee tool to define the selection area.

Set the width of the selection to exactly one-third of the current selection (one-third of 300 equals 100 pixels). Set the height to 2 pixels.

Step 2.

Click once on the bottom left corner of the plank to select an area that is 100 pixels wide and 2 pixels deep.

You will use this selected area as a guide to placing your plank elements when creating your pattern. You will have to add some color to this selection so that you can see it after you deselect it.

Step 3.

Hide the selection marquee by choosing **Hide Edges** from the **Select** menu.

Step 4.

Now add some color to the selection. Choose **Brightness/Contrast** from the **Adjust** submenu of the **Image** menu (or press Command-B). Alternatively, you could also choose **Fill** from the **Edit** menu to fill the selection area with the foreground color.

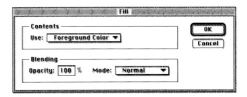

Step 5.

Nudge the selection down a pixel or two away from the plank using the down-arrow key. The space that this creates between the objects will help you place the next object in the pattern.

Step 6.

You may want to enlarge the view of the image to see the changes you're making better. To do this, you can either click once on the image with the Zoom tool or use the keyboard shortcut Command-+.

Step 7.

Next, you have to place the next plank in the pattern. Choose **Paste** from the **Edit** menu (or press Command-V).

Step 8.

Move the new plank into position so that the right edge of the plank is lined up exactly with the right edge of the location guide that you just created with the selection tool.

Step 9.

Use the up-arrow cursor key to nudge the new plank into place, one pixel at a time, until it rests against the bottom edge of the existing plank.

Step 10.

It's time to clone the object you just pasted. While the plank is still selected, hold down the Option key and click the plank. Click and hold down the mouse button and drag the selection to the right to create a perfect duplicate of the plank.

Step 11.

Place the new plank so that its left edge rests against the right edge of the previous copy.

Step 12.

Select the Rectangular Marquee tool and click the bottom right corner of the newly placed clone.

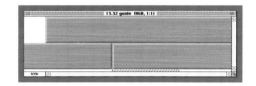

Step 13.

Change the color of the selection using the same technique you used in the previous steps.

Step 14.

Paste in another copy of the plank by choosing **Paste** from the **Edit** menu.

Step 15.

Use the guide you just created to place the right edge of the new selection over the right edge of the space guide.

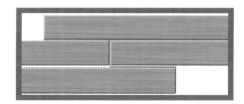

Step 16.

Choose **Hide Edges** from the **Select** menu and use the cursor keys to nudge the plank into position.

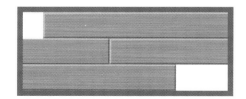

Step 17.

Finally, create another copy of the current selection by holding down the Option key while you drag the selection to the right. Place the left edge of the cloned object against the right edge of the last plank. It might help to hide the edges of your selection by choosing **Hide Edges** under the **Select** menu.

The next part of the process is to define the pattern. Follow these steps:

Step 1.

Using the Rectangular Marquee tool, select all three rows of planks, using the top plank as a corner guide. An easy way to do this is to double-click on the Rectangular Marquee tool and type the appropriate values in the Fixed Size fields to create a defined selection area.

Remember, the original plank dimensions were 300 by 40 pixels, so the selection area you want to define now will have the same width and be three times as deep.

Step 2.

Set the Fixed Size fields to 300 pixels wide by 120 pixels deep.

Step 3.

Using the Rectangular Marquee tool, click on the top right corner of the original wood plank to select the part of the image you want to use to define the pattern.

This a good place to save this new element to your library of textures and patterns. Copy the selection using the **Copy** command from the **File** menu. Then, choose **New** from the **File** menu. Notice how the new document has exactly the same parameters as the copied image on the clipboard. Paste the copied object into this new document and save it in your working folder.

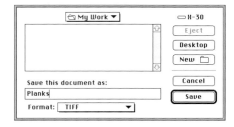

Then, save and close the document.

Let's add a little variety to the work in progress:

Step 1.

The selected area is still active in the image, so choose **90° CW** from the **Rotate** submenu of the **Image** menu to rotate the pattern tile.

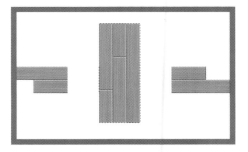

Step 2.

Choose **Inverse** from the **Select** menu and press the Delete key to delete everything except the pattern tile. Then choose **Inverse** from the **Select** menu again to reselect the pattern tile.

Step 3.

Choose **Define Pattern** from the **Edit** menu to define this area as a pattern tile.

Step 4.

Choose **All** from the **Select** menu (or use the keyboard shortcut Command-A).

Step 5.

Choose **Fill** from the **Edit** menu. Make sure that Pattern is selected from the pull-down menu and the opacity is 100%.

Step 6.

Click OK to fill the entire area with the new pattern.

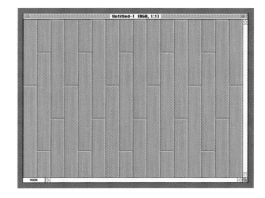

Very impressive (and easy)!

Wait—there's more! Remember, you can change the color of the filled pattern on the fly as you're working. There are a couple of easy ways to accomplish this. You can choose **Hue/Saturation** from the **Adjust** submenu of the **Image** menu (keyboard shortcut Command-U),or choose **Brightness/Contrast** from the **Adjust** submenu of the **Image** menu (keyboard shortcut Command-B).

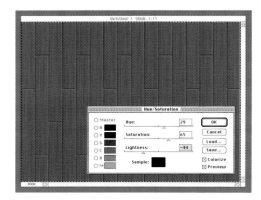

Your finished work should look pretty similar to this. Be sure to save it into the working folder as a library texture to use later. Now let's move on to a slightly more detailed pattern.

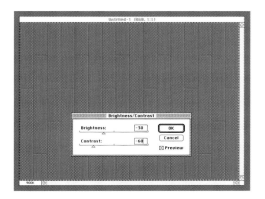

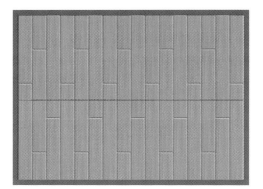

Creating Parquet

In this section, you learn about an interesting variation of the wood pattern technique that you can use to create a parquet pattern. It's fairly simple to produce because the pattern elements are symmetrical and easy to reproduce. You can make the pattern as simple or complex as you like.

This technique is a great addition to your texture library. You can recolor and resize the pattern tiles in an incredible number of ways to fit your illustration requirements.

To create a parquet pattern, follow these steps:

Step 1.

Create a new document measuring 640 by 480 pixels in RGB Color mode with a resolution of 72 pixels/inch.

Step 2.

Open one of your favorite wood textures that you have already created. Try using the wood plank from the previous section.

Step 3.

Choose **All** from the **Select** menu.

Step 4.

Choose **Copy** from the **Edit** menu.

Step 5.

Close the wood plank document.

Step 6.

Choose **Paste** from the **Edit** menu to paste the wood plank into the new document.

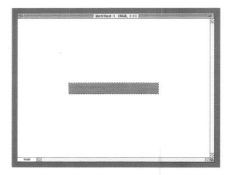

The object of this technique is to create a new pattern out of an existing pattern. Each pattern tile will consist of 16 adjacent planks that you assemble by pasting and copying. The pattern will look like this when complete.

As you can see, four planks laid side by side must occupy the same horizontal space as the length of a single plank. You must reduce the length of a single plank to exactly the width of four planks.

Follow these steps:

Step 1.

Choose **Show Info** from the **Window** menu to display the Info palette.

You use the Info palette as a guide to determine how short to make your plank. The width and height of the selection are shown at the bottom of the palette. You need to make the length of the plank four times the height. Since the height of the plank is 40 pixels, the length must be 160 pixels.

Step 2.

Choose **Scale** from the **Effects** submenu of the **Image** menu.

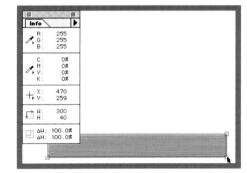

Step 3.

Drag one of the handles from right to left to reduce the length of the plank to 160 pixels. Be careful not to change the height of the plank, it should remain at 40 pixels.

Click inside the selection to stamp it in place.

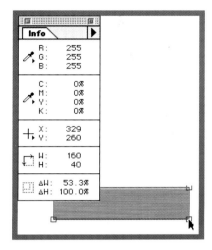

So far, so good. Now, you need to duplicate the plank three times to create a simple pattern. Follow these steps:

Step 1.

Hold down the Option and Shift keys while you click on and drag the selection straight down to make a clone of it.

Step 2.

Place the clone next to the bottom edge of the existing plank.

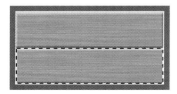

It might help to enlarge the view (by pressing Command-+) and hide the edges of the selection marquee (by pressing Command-H) to better see the changes you're making.

Step 3.

Repeat steps 1 and 2 two more times to finish the process.

To finish the pattern tile, follow these steps:

Step 1.

Double-click the Rectangular Marquee tool. Click the Fixed Sized radio button and set both the vertical and horizontal settings to 160 pixels. This will define a fixed size selection area.

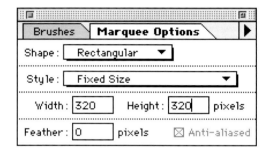

Step 2.

Select all four planks at once by clicking the top left corner of the assembly.

Step 3.

Copy the selection by choosing **Copy** from the **Edit** menu (or by pressing Command-C).

Step 4.

Paste in a new selection by choosing **Paste** from the **Edit** menu (or by pressing Command-V).

Step 5.

Move the newly pasted selection up and2 to the right so that the bottom left corner rests against the top right corner of the existing image.

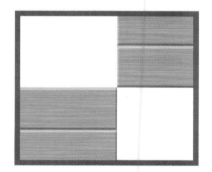

It might help to hide the edges of the selection (by pressing Command-H) and enlarge the view (by pressing Command-+).

Step 6.

Add the rest of the design by pasting in another element. Choose **Paste** from the **Edit** menu (or press Command-V).

Step 7.

Next, you need to change the direction of the planks. Choose **90° CW** from the **Rotate** submenu of the **Image** menu.

Step 8.

Drag the image into position using the mouse.

Once again, it might help to hide the edges of the selection marquee (Command-H) and enlarge the view (Command-+). Remember, you can nudge the selection one pixel at a time by using the arrow keys.

Step 9.

Choose **Horizontal** from the **Flip** submenu of the **Image** menu. This keeps the light source consistent for the planks.

Step 10.

Clone this piece by holding down the Option key while you click and drag up and to the left.

Step 11.

Position the clone in the blank upper left quadrant of the pattern.

Step 12.

Now select the entire pattern. This is easy if you use the old trick of defining a fixed size for the selection. You know that the dimensions of the object are twice those of your last selection, so double-click the Rectangular Marquee tool to define a fixed size of 320 by 320 pixels.

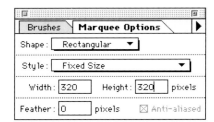

Step 13.

Click the upper left corner of the object to select the entire tile. Because the Rectangular Marquee tool is set to select exactly 320 by 320 pixels, you can select the entire object by itself with one click.

Here's another good stopping place to copy the object and save it into another document. Choose **Copy** from the **Edit** menu. Choose **New** from the **File** menu. Then, choose **Paste** from the **Edit** menu. Close the document, remembering to name it something creative like "Parquet."

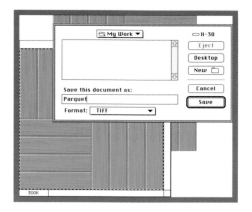

Back to the original document. The selected area looks like it might be a tad too big to use as a basis for a pattern. Use the following steps to reduce its size to something a little more reasonable:

Step 1.

Choose **Scale** from the **Effects** submenu of the **Image** menu.

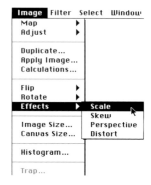

Step 2.

Press and hold the Shift key while you click on and drag the upper right handle down to the center of the selection, where the pattern tiles converge.

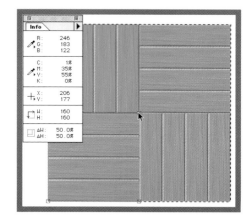

This makes a pattern tile that is 50 percent the size of the original. The divisions between the elements (and the Info palette) act as convenient guides for making this change.

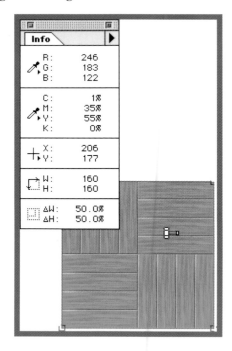

You can see how the info palette shows the degree of reduction in percent at the bottom of the palette.

You can test the technique as follows:

Step 1.

Choose **Define Pattern** from the **Edit** menu.

Step 2.

Choose **All** from the **Select** menu (or press Command-A).

Step 3.

Choose **Fill** from the **Edit** menu to fill the selected area with the new pattern.

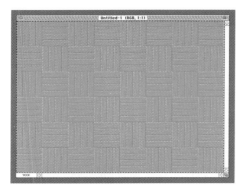

You can make some fine adjustments to enhance the image. While the filled area is still selected, choose **Unsharp Mask...** from the **Sharpen** submenu of the **Filter** menu. This will add some fine details to the image.

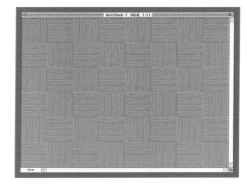

And that's concludes a basic introduction to many of the tools and techniques we'll use in the rest of the book. Along the way, you've created some great background textures you can use in your everyday projects. In the following chapter, we'll create some new textures you can use in much the same way.

Creating a Brushed
Aluminum Texture

page 30

Creating a
Diamond Plate
Corrugated
Metal Pattern

page 32

Enhancing
and
Weathering

page 35

Adding Rust
Textures to
an Object

page 37

Adding
Ornaments

page 42

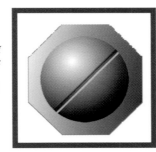

Chapter 2

Metallic Textures

Metallic textures are unique and easy to produce. In this chapter, you'll learn how to apply simple noise and blur filters, graduated blends, and colorizations to simulate a variety of real-looking metals.

Photoshop's painting tools are easy to use, and they enable you to create some stunning textural effects. The exercises in this chapter show you the basics of creating a variety of metallic textures from brushed aluminum to rusting metal. The secret is using some common filters under the Filter menu.

Later on, you will apply additional layers of texture to simulate aging and weathered metal effects.

These metallic textures can be dramatic as backgrounds or even as objects themselves. They also make great interior textures for technical renderings, visualizations, letter forms, and type objects.

Creating a Brushed Aluminum Texture

This technique uses simple noise filters and blur filters to achieve a real-looking metallic brushed aluminum texture. Like the wood grains and wood paneling textures, you can color and adjust the contrast of this texture to simulate a variety of other metal textures. You can add your own little enhancements to give it that extra touch.

Follow these steps:

Step 1.

Create a new document measuring 640 by 480 pixels in RGB Color mode, with a resolution of 72 pixels/inch.

Step 2.

Fill the entire area with a uniform gaussian noise. Choose **Add Noise** from the **Noise** submenu of the **Filter** menu. Set the amount to 999.

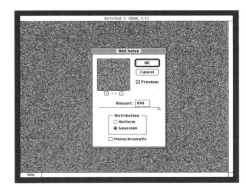

You don't have to make a selection to apply the filter. No selection is active, so the filter is applied to the entire document area.

Step 3.

Choose **Motion Blur** from the **Blur** submenu of the **Filter** menu. Set the angle to 90° and the distance to 120.

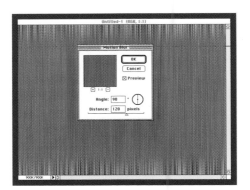

An effective technique, but not quite perfect. Notice how the top and bottom edges of the image area are contrasty streaks. This image needs more work. Follow these steps:

Step 1.

Using the Rectangular Marquee tool, select an area in the interior; be sure to avoid the streaks along the edges.

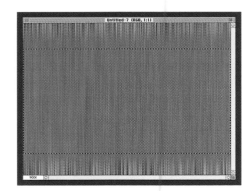

Step 2.

Choose **Crop** from the **Edit** menu to reduce the image area to the selection area.

You now have a perfectly workable new metallic texture, and created in only five simple steps. You can adjust the color levels and apparent contrast. Choose **Hue/Saturation** from the **Adjust** submenu of the **Image** menu. Experiment with entering different values in the **Hue/Saturation** dialog box.

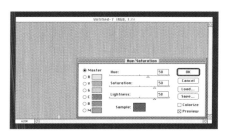

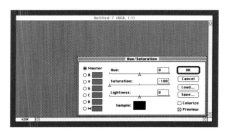

You can make this texture even better by adding some life to the image using the Gradient tool.

Step 1.

Customize the Gradient tool settings by double-clicking the tool. Change the values by clicking the appropriate radio buttons as pictured below. Make sure that the Linear button is selected.

Also, make sure that the foreground color is set to black and the background color is set to white. (The shortcut for this is to click the Default Colors icon in the lower left corner of the tool palette.)

Step 2.

Now reverse the foreground and background colors by clicking on the Switch Colors icon in the upper right of the swatch area. This makes white the foreground color and black the background color.

Step 3.

Choose **Show Brushes** from the **Window** menu to display the brushes palette. Make sure your opacity is set to 30% and the mode to Darken.

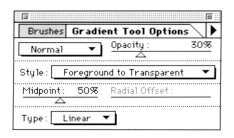

Step 4.

With the Gradient tool still selected, click in the center of the image. Now hold down the Shift key as you drag the cursor to the left across the image. This adds a subtle blending of shade across the width of the image.

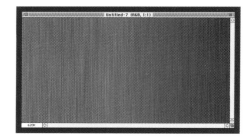

This is a nice enhancement, but you're not quite there yet. Let's add one more effect to enhance the look.

Step 5.

Change the mode on the Brushes palette to Lighten.

Step 6.

With the gradient tool still selected, click in the center of the image. Now hold down the Shift key as you drag the cursor to the left.

There, now you're ready to save this texture to the library of textures folder. Choose **Save** from the **File** menu and name this document "Brushed Metal."

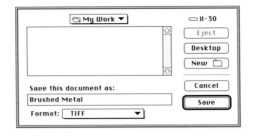

Don't forget: you can adjust the color intensities by choosing **Hue/Saturation** from the **Adjust** submenu of the **Image** menu.

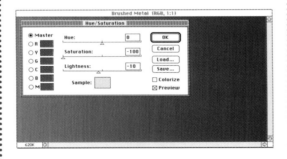

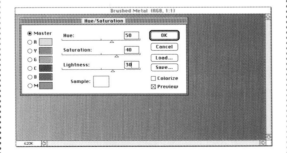

Creating a Diamond Plate Corrugated Metal Pattern

This section presents a great effect you can create to simulate a diamond-plate metallic finish. You can use this texture to give an industrial flavor to an illustration. It's simple to produce, and you can easily add life to the texture by giving it a shiny new finish or a rusty and weathered feeling.

The diamond plate corrugated texture looks great as a background or as a texture you can apply to text or three-dimensional objects. Be sure to save this new texture in your library.

To create the diamond plate corrugated metal texture, follow these steps:

Step 1.

Create a new document measuring 640 by 480 pixels in RGB Color mode with a 72 pixel/inch resolution.

Step 2.

Use the Rectangular Marquee tool to create a selection measuring about two inches square. (Remember, you can constrain the creation of a selection shape by holding down the Shift key while you drag with the selection tool).

Step 3.

Fill this area with black. Remember the shortcut for changing the swatche's to black and white is to click the Switch Colors icon in the lower left corner near the color swatch selection area.

Step 4.

Choose **Arbitrary...** from the **Effects** submenu of the **Rotate** menu. Rotate the selection 45°CW.

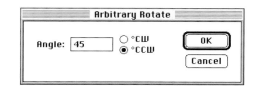

Step 5.

Choose **Scale** from the **Effects** submenu of the **Image** menu to make the selection very tall and narrow.

Step 6.

Hold down the Option key, and then click and drag to move a clone of this tall diamond shape to the right. (You could also choose **Copy** and **Paste** from the **Edit** menu, but why add extra steps for such a simple operation?)

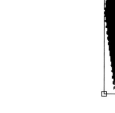

Step 7.

While the new tall diamond shape is selected, choose **90°CW** from the **Rotate** submenu of the **Image** menu. This will 90°CW to rotate the second diamond shape perpendicular to the original tall diamond shape.

Step 8.

If the second diamond shape is close enough to the original that they are touching (or almost touching), click to select it and then drag it away from the original, leaving enough distance between them so that you can make an evenly spaced pattern from them later.

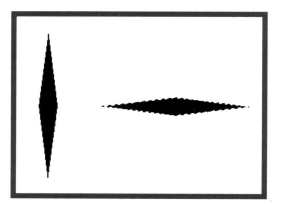

You need to space these apart by about a third of their length. Also, make sure that the end point of the horizontal diamond is lined up with the side point of the vertical diamond. This ensures that the diamond pattern you create will align correctly later.

Step 9.

Next, use the Magic Wand tool to select the remaining unselected diamond shape.

Both pieces should now be selected (you will see the "marching ants" around both diamonds signifying that they are selected).

Step 10.

Choose **Arbitrary…** from the **Rotate** submenu of the the **Image** menu. Rotate both pieces 45°CCW.

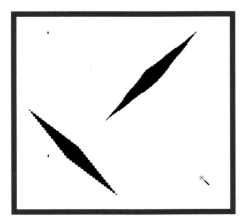

Step 11.

With all the selecting and manipulating you have done, a few selection artifacts may be visible in the working area. To get rid of these, choose **Inverse** from the **Select** menu and delete the color out of the new selection by pressing the Delete key.

Note: When you press the Delete key, whatever color is contained in the selection is replaced by the current background color.

Step 12.

Hold down the Shift key and use the Rectangular Marquee tool to drag a perfectly square selection around the two tall diamond shapes. Start at the top right corner, where the point of the uppermost diamond shape starts, and drag to the opposite corner, being sure to include both shapes in the selection area. Try not to select too much area outside the shapes.

This is a great place to stop for a moment to save this element as a basis for a new texture later. Choose **Copy** from the **Edit** menu (or press Command-C). Choose **New** from the **File** menu to create a new document into which to paste the current selection. Note that the New Document dialog box has parameters listed that are equal to the area you have copied to the Clipboard.

Choose **Paste** from the **Edit** menu (or press Command-V) to paste the selection into the new document. Next, choose **Save** from the **File** menu and name the new document "Diamond Plate Basis."

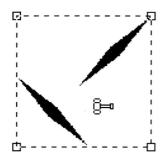

Now that you have saved this pattern tile document, you can close it and get back to the work at hand:

Step 1.

Choose **Scale** from the **Effects** submenu of the **Image** menu. Drag the scale handles to shrink the selection by about 50 percent. Make sure that you scale the selection proportionally by holding down the Shift key while you drag the scale handles.

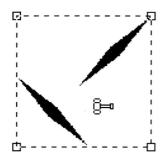

Step 2.

Choose **Define Pattern** from the **Edit** menu to make the selection a pattern tile.

Step 3.

Now all you have to do is select the entire image area (or any other image area that you can select, including type objects or any Lasso or Magic Wand selection) and choose **Fill** from the **Edit** menu to fill the selected area with the pattern.

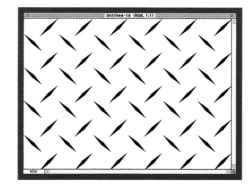

Step 4.

To finish off the basic effect, choose **Emboss** from the **Stylize** submenu of the **Filter** menu.

Step 5.

Set the Emboss parameters to 90°, 1 pixel height, and 100%.

Voilà! A perfect gray diamond plate pattern!

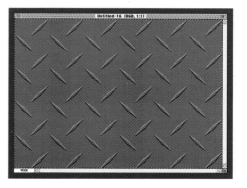

Weathering the Diamond Plate Pattern

You can enhance the diamond plate pattern by adding a rougher texture or some weathering and rust. Enhancements like these work best when applied overall to the entire image area rather than to just a single pattern tile. You want the effect to appear uniformly across the entire selection. But, if you apply rust or a rough texture to a single tile and then create a pattern fill from that tile, you will see a line dividing each pattern tile.

Follow these steps:

Step 1.

Start by selecting all the gray pixels in the document. Do this by clicking on a gray area with the Magic Wand tool, and then choosing **Similar** from the **Select** menu.

Step 2.

Choose **Add Noise** from the **Noise** submenu of the **Filter** menu. Choose gaussian blur and set the amount to 16 to add a somewhat subtle mottling to the entire area.

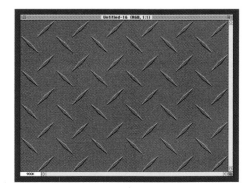

Not bad so far. This would almost be enough texture by removing color values or coloring the selection, but you can make the selection a bit more rough.

Step 3.

Choose **Emboss** from the **Stylize** submenu of the **Filter** menu.

You can also use the keyboard shortcut Command-F to reapply the previous filter. Pressing Command-F applies the same filter with the same value settings used previously.

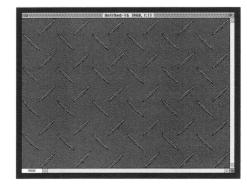

Wow! Now *this* looks good!

Enhancing the Effect

You can enhance any of these looks by adding some of the special effects you have already learned and others that you are about to learn. Follow the steps in the following section on rusting and weathered metals to make the diamond plate look oxidized and worn. You also might try adding varying layers of rust.

Another more subtle effect is to add a light gradient tint to the selection. Select the entire area and use the Gradient tool to add a linear graduation to the diamond plate texture. Experiment with changing the settings in the Brushes palette to lighten, darken, or multiply the opacity value.

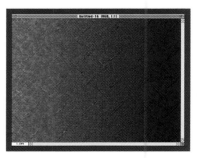

Adding Rust Textures to an Object

In this section, you learn how to add some weathering effects to artificially age a metallic texture. You learn some simple filter and selection techniques to add realistic-looking rust textures to any object.

The effect is simple to produce, relying mostly on Noise filters and colorization to achieve a very real weathered effect. You will love the way it can be enhanced using the emboss filter to add a subtle but dramatic dimensionality to the effect. Best of all, you can apply this technique to any Photoshop illustration quickly and easily.

Follow these steps:

Step 1.

Create a new document measuring 640 by 480 pixels in RGB Color mode with a 72 pixel/inch resolution.

Now you need to add some kind of shape to texturize. Keep in mind that you can add this texture to anything you can select. Because it doesn't have to be a rectangular or elliptical shape, you can just as easily apply this texture to selected letter forms or anything that the Magic Wand tool can select. For this example, you will add rust to some basic letter forms.

Step 2.

Click on the Type tool and click once in the center of the image area.

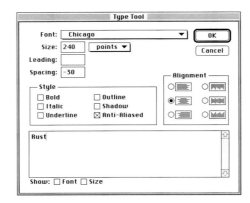

Step 3.

Create some letters using the Chicago font. This exercise uses the Chicago font because it is a simple, generic, scalable font that is automatically present on any Macintosh system. Any scalable font that will appear smooth at a larger size is fine to use.

Step 4.

In the type specifications dialog box that appears, enable anti-aliasing, set the alignment to centered, and set the spacing to any comfortable amount depending on the typeface you have chosen.

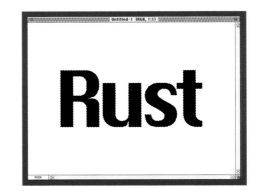

Next, you need to add some color or texture to this selected text shape. In this exercise, instead of defining a flat color, you add a subtle gradation using the Gradient tool.

Step 5.

Double-click the Gradient tool in the Tool palette. Select the Linear mode radio button in the Gradient Tool specification dialog box. Make sure the style is set to Normal and the midpoint skew is 50%.

Step 6.

Choose **Show Brushes** from the **Window** menu to display the Brushes palette. Make sure that the painting mode is set to Lighten and the opacity is set to 50%. This ensures that the graduation will cover the selection completely.

Step 7.

With the Gradient tool selected, click at the vertical midpoint of the letters. Then drag upwards across the letters to apply a graduation in the selected areas.

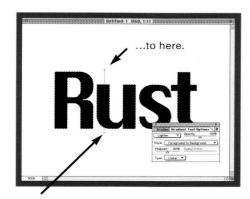

...to here.

Drag up from here...

If it doesn't look right the first time, you can always choose **Undo** from the **Edit** menu and try again until you achieve the effect you want. Because most of the area that is selected will be covered by a rusty texture, it's not imperative that this layer look absolutely perfect.

Tip: If you want to be really creative, why not add a simple brushed metal texture to this selection as described in the previous section? This can greatly enhance the realism of the technique. Remember, you can apply the rusty texture over anything you can select.

Now that some of the basics are accomplished, let's attend to some of the mechanics of this effect.

Step 8.

Choose **Show Channels** from the **Window** menu.

Step 9.

In the Channel palette, choose the New Channel option twice to create two new channels.

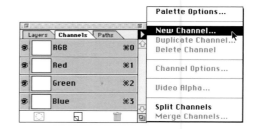

Notice that in each of these new channels, the letter shapes in the RGB channel are still selected.

Step 10.

In each of these channels, choose **Fill** from the **Edit** menu and fill the selections with the foreground color (black).

Step 11.

Go to channel 4. Choose **Add Noise** from the **Noise** submenu of the **Filter** menu. Set the amount to 999 for maximum random pixel noise and click the Gaussian distribution radio button.

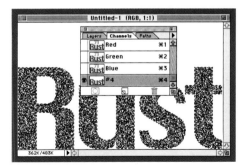

Remember, the image in the additional channels will always display as grayscale.

Step 12.

To roughen up the noise, choose **Diffuse** from the **Stylize** submenu of the **Filter** menu. Set the mode to Normal.

Notice how this filter scatters and diffuses the pixels just a bit. Reapply this filter 10 more times using the keyboard shortcut Command-F.

You can make this image as rough as you like by reapplying the filter until you get the effect that looks best to you. But, once you have the look you want, don't reapply the filter any more. You will see why in a few steps.

Step 13.

Choose **None** from the **Select** menu (or press Command-D) to deselect the selection in this channel.

Step 14.

Choose the Magic Wand tool and click once on a darker area.

Step 15.

Choose **Similar** from the **Select** menu to select the rest of the black pixels in this channel.

Time to return to the RGB channel, if only briefly, to begin applying your magic touch to the image.

Step 16.

In the Channels palette, click the RGB name (or press Command-0) to return to the RGB channel. You will see that the Magic Wand selection you made in the extra channel is still selected in the RGB channel.

Step 17.

Choose **Feather** from the **Select** menu and set the feather radius to 3 pixels.

Step 18.

Choose **Hide Edges** from the **Select** menu to hide the "marching ants" around the selected pixels.

Step 19.

To add a nice basic blended rusty color, simply colorize the selection. Choose **Hue/Saturation** from the **Adjust** submenu of the **Image** menu. Click the Colorize and Preview check boxes in the resulting dialog box. Set the values to Hue: 30, Saturation: 50, and Lightness: -30.

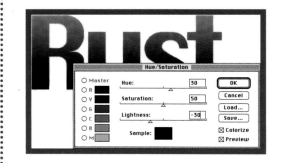

This is a basic background rust that should serve as a mild form of iron oxidation. You can add it to any selected object or texture.

Let's enhance the effect a bit by adding more texture to the rust. Follow these steps:

Step 1.

Go back to the fourth channel. Choose the Magic Wand tool and click once on a darker area. Choose **Similar** from the **Select** menu to select the rest of the black pixels in this channel.

Step 2.

Return to the RGB channel by using the keyboard shortcut Command-0.

Since you haven't chosen to feather the selection, all the selected areas have a harder edge. You can hide the edges using the **Hide Edges** command from the **Select** menu to get a clearer picture of the next adjustment you make to these pixels.

Step 3.

Choose **Hue/Saturation** from the **Adjust** submenu of the **Image** menu (or press **Command-U**). Once again, make sure that the Colorize and Preview check boxes are selected and set the values to Hue: 30, Saturation: 60, and Lightness: 0.

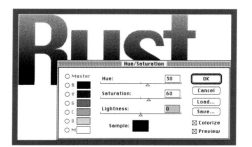

This procedure lends a little more texture to the effect, making it appear more real. Layering the effects from subtle to extreme in steps can enhance any texture. Remember this point as you go forth in your Photoshop adventures.

Although this is a nice effect in its own right, sometimes you need to create an even crustier, more corroded rust effect. Lucky for us, it's an easy step to apply:

Step 1.

While the rusted areas are still selected (even though the selection edges are hidden), choose **Emboss** from the **Stylize** submenu of **Filter** menu.

Step 2.

Set the values in the dialog box to angle: 135°, depth: 1 pixel, and amount: 100%.

This produces an interesting effect. It adds some contrast to the edges of the selected pixels, adds some gray iron coloring to the interiors, and leaves some rust coloring around the edges. A powerful technique, but let's enhance it further by colorizing the selection.

Step 3.

Choose **Hue/Saturation** from the **Adjust** submenu of the **Image** menu. Adjust the sliders to add some rust coloring to the selected embossed areas. Try setting the values to Hue: 30, Saturation: 70, and Lightness: 0.

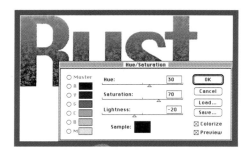

Step 4.

Make the rust even crustier by reapplying the Emboss filter and repeating the colorizing step.

Step 5.

You can enhance it further by choosing **Brightness/Contrast** from the **Adjust** submenu of the **Image** menu (or use the keyboard shortcut Command-B).

Now it's time for cleanup. Here's where the fifth channel comes into play:

Step 1.

Go to the fifth channel. Choose the Magic Wand tool and click once on a darker area. Choose **Similar** from the **Select** menu to select the rest of the black pixels in this channel.

Step 2.

Return to the RGB channel and, choose **Inverse** from the **Select** menu.

Step 3.

Your objective is to remove any colored pixels outside of the text. While all the inverted outside pixels are selected, press the Delete key to remove everything outside of the text, leaving just the background color.

Tip: If the background color is set to anything other than white, when you press that Delete key, the entire background will turn to that color. If this happens, just click once on the Default Colors icon in the tool palette, to set the foreground and background colors to black and white, and then press the Delete key again.

Step 4.

Finally, add the finishing touch by choosing **Inverse** from the **Select** menu to re-select the artwork.

Step 5.

Choose **Stroke** from the **Edit** menu. Set the Stroke weight to 4 pixels, the opacity to 100%, the mode to Normal, and the location to Center.

Step 6.

Click OK. You will see the hard-won effect all cleaned up and neat with a thick defining border around the letters.

This is a wonderful technique that looks realistic and only took you a few minutes to complete. The best part is that it didn't require much handiwork, just the application of simple filters and effects. You may want to save it now for future reference.

Tip: You can save file space by choosing PICT as a file format. It doesn't support extra channels, thereby reducing the memory requirements.

An interesting experiment would be to use a macro utility to assign the entire rusting process a simple one-key application. The animation that this produces would be striking, and it would look great in multi-media presentations.

Adding Ornaments to Enhance the Metallic Effect

This section presents a few tips for adding some simple environmental ornaments to help enhance a metallic effect. The premise is that there's a relational assumption of an object's identity based on the details of the environment. Basically, this means that an egg is more readily identifiable if there's a chicken nearby. In this instance, the metallic effect is more recognizable as such with some ornaments like nuts, bolts, screws, and rust.

In this section, you create some ornaments that you will save as individual documents that you can draw from whenever you need them.

Flathead Screws

Let's start with a few loose screws.

Step 1.

Create a new document that's relatively small compared with other documents you have created so far. Make this document 200 by 200 pixels in RGB Color mode, with a resolution of 72 pixels/inch.

Step 2.

Screws have a round, flat face, so you need to use the Elliptical Marquee tool to select a perfectly round area. Hold down the Shift key while you drag the cursor from the upper left corner down to the lower right.

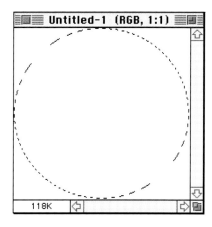

Step 3.

Next, add a subtle shading and texture to the selection. Choose **Add Noise** from the **Noise** submenu of the **Filter** menu. Set the amount to 111 and choose Gaussian distribution.

Step 4.

Choose **Motion Blur** from the **Blur** submenu of the **Filter** menu. Set the blur to any angle and set the distance to 120. This should give a very subtle streaking to the face of the screw. If you want to enhance the streaks, repeat the filter by using the keyboard shortcut Command-F.

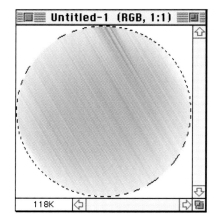

Step 5.

If you want to add one more subtle effect, double-click the Gradient tool. Set the style to a linear blend.

Step 6.

Choose **Show Brushes** from the **Window** menu. Set the opacity of the gradient tool to 30% and the mode to Darken.

Step 7.

With the Gradient tool selected, drag diagonally across the selection from the bottom right corner to the upper left corner.

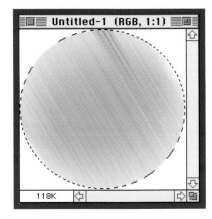

You may want to apply the gradation in a few different ways by choosing different modes in the Brushes palette. Try Multiply and Lighten for starters.

Next, you need to add the slot for the screwdriver. You do this by using the Line tool and choosing contrasting hues of the metallic gray color to indicate the highlighted and shadowed side of the screw slot. Follow these steps:

Step 1.

Make sure that the foreground and background colors use the default black and white by clicking on the Default Colors icon in the lower right corner of the tool palette.

Step 2.

Choose the Line tool.

Step 3.

You can define the width of the line by double-clicking it and changing the width setting in pixels. For this exercise, set the width to 4. Make sure that the Line Tool option is set to 50% opacity and the mode is set to Normal.

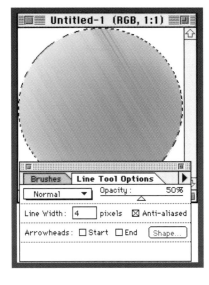

Step 4.

Press and hold down the Shift key as you drag diagonally up from the lower left corner of the selection.

Holding down the Shift key constrains the Line tool to drawing a perfect 45° angle. Since you have a marquee selection active, the stroke appears only within the area of the selection. And since the Brushes palette is set to only 50% opacity, the shadowed side of the screw slot has a subtle shade.

You can accent the shadowed line you just made by creating another line right on top of it or one pixel to the right or left. Because the opacity is set to 50%, you're enhancing the existing pixels and adding faint pixels right beside them. It's a subtle effect that adds a bit of realism to the style.

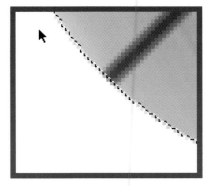

You add the highlighted side of the screwdriver slot the same way you added the shaded side. Follow these steps:

Step 1.

To reverse the color swatch selection, click the Switch Colors icon in the upper right corner of the color swatch area. You don't need to adjust the mode or opacity in the Brushes palette because they're already set.

Step 2.

Drag the Line tool to create a new line, starting a few pixels to the right of the original, darker line.

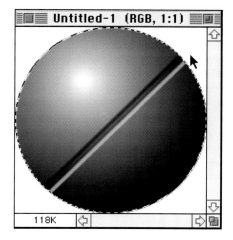

Step 3.

Consider the light source and add another highlighted line the same way you accented the shadowed line.

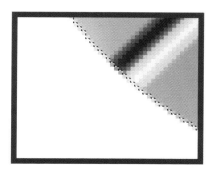

Step 4.

Wasn't that easy? Before deselecting the round screw area, choose **Save** from the **File** menu and save this document into your working library folder.

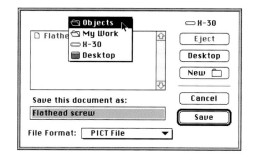

Tip: Although you have saved the screw as a large object in the working folder, you will always want to reduce the size of this item before adding it elsewhere. This will blend the pixels a bit and add realism to the illustration.

Roundhead Screws

This section presents a similar technique that you can use to create excellent little roundhead screws to enhance metal effects. It uses the same basic technique (with one little difference) as the flathead screws. Follow these steps:

Step 1.

Start by creating a new document measuring 200 by 200 pixels in RGB Color mode, with a resolution of 72 pixels/inch.

Step 2.

Use the Elliptical Marquee tool to select a perfectly round area that almost fills the area of the picture.

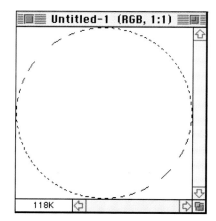

Remember, you can constrain the width and height of any new shape to equal proportions by holding down the Shift key while you draw it.

Step 3.

Instead of adding gaussian noise for texture, add a radial gradient fill. Double-click the Gradient tool to set the mode to Radial. If the Brushes palette is visible and shows settings from the last demonstration, set the mode to Normal and the opacity to 100%. Now, make sure that the foreground and background colors are set to white and black. Drag diagonally across the round selection from a point in the upper left area.

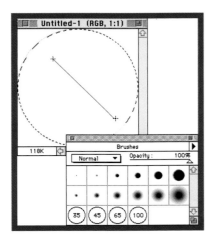

Step 4.

Make sure that the foreground and background colors are the default black and white by clicking on the Default Colors icon in the lower left corner of the tool palette.

Step 5.

Choose the Line tool. You can define the width of the line by double-clicking it and changing the width setting in pixels. For this exercise, set the width to 4 pixels. Make sure that the Brushes palette is set to 50% opacity and the mode is set to Normal.

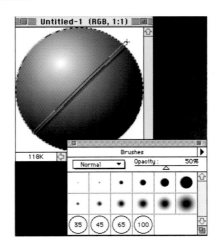

Step 6.

Press and hold down the Shift key as you drag diagonally up from the lower left corner of the selection.

Holding down the Shift key constrains the Line tool to drawing a perfect 45° angle. Because you have a marquee selection active, the stroke appears only within the area of the selection. And because the Brushes palette is set to only 50% opacity, the shadowed side of the screw slot has a subtle shade.

You can accent the shadowed line you just made by creating another line right on top of it or one pixel to the right or left. Because the opacity is set to 50%, you're enhancing the existing pixels and adding faint pixels right beside them. It's a subtle effect that adds a bit of realism to the style. Try adding a line or two next to the original lines to add some weight to the slot.

Remember, if you hold down the Shift key while you create these lines, they will be constrained and, therefore, parallel when you create them.

You add the highlighted side of the screwdriver slot the same way you added the shaded side. Follow these steps:

Step 1.

To reverse the foreground and background colors, click the Switch Colors icon in the upper right corner of the color swatch area. You don't need to adjust the mode or opacity in the Brushes palette because they're already set.

Step 2.

Drag the line tool cursor to create a new line, starting a few pixels to the right of the original darker line.

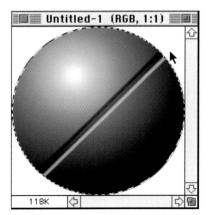

Step 3.

Consider the light source and add another highlighted line the same way you accented the shadowed line.

Step 4.

Before deselecting the round screw area, choose **Save** from the **File** menu and save this document into your working library folder.

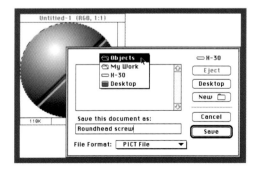

Bolts and Nuts

How many times (in the last week alone) have you wondered to yourself, "How can I, an ordinary illustrator, make a perfect octagon using Adobe Photoshop?" This and many mysteries like it have baffled scientists for years. Here at last, at no additional cost or obligation, is the long-sought-after secret of creating perfect octagons. It's easy, and all it takes is a few simple steps using the Rectangular Marquee tool. Follow these steps:

Step 1.

Create a new document measuring 400 by 400 pixels in RGB Color mode, with a resolution of 72 pixels/inch.

Step 2.

Use the Rectangular Marquee tool to select a perfectly square area near the center of the image.

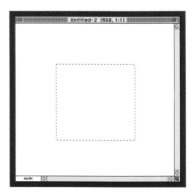

Hold down the Shift key while you drag the selection tool to constrain the dimensions to equal proportions.

Tip: You can control and define the exact area that the Rectangular Marquee tool will select by double-clicking the tool and choosing a fixed size in the Options dialog box.

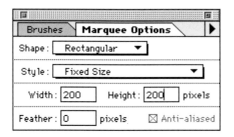

Step 3.

Choose **Copy** from the **Edit** menu.

Step 4.

Choose **Arbitrary...** from the **Rotate** submenu of the Image menu. Set angle to 45°.

Step 5.

Now for the fun and mysterious part. Choose **Paste Into** from the **Edit** menu.

Step 6.

Choose **Fill** from the **Edit** menu and fill the selection with 100% of the black foreground color.

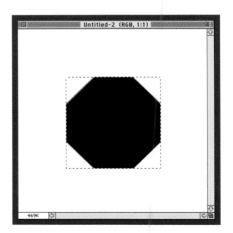

Step 7.

Aha, the perfect octagon! Choose the Magic Wand tool and click once on the center of the octagon to select it.

Hint: if you set the tolerance of the Wand tool to a fairly high level (around 64), you're sure to select all the associated pixels.

Now you can copy the octagon into another new document, or start adding special effects to texturize it.

Now to add a subtle shaded gray tint of metal to the shape.

Follow these steps:

Step 1.

While the octagon is still selected, choose the Gradient tool.

Step 2.

Set the Brush palette settings to 100% opacity and Normal mode. Also, set the foreground and background colors to white and black.

Step 3.

With the Gradient tool selected, drag diagonally across the selected area, starting outside the selection and finishing outside the boundaries of the selection.

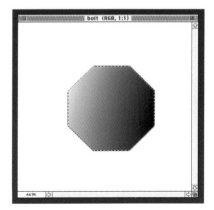

Step 4.

You may want to dress up the bolt with a roundhead screw pasted right into the center of it. Open the roundhead screw document and copy it. Then paste it directly onto the bolt.

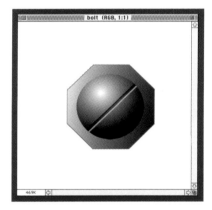

There now. A nice, free-for-the-taking bolt and screw ornament that you can add to the library.

Step 5.

Select the ornament by choosing the Magic Wand tool and clicking once in the background. Then, choose **Inverse** from the **Select** menu.

Step 6.

Choose **Copy** from the **Edit** menu.

Step 7.

Create a new document, paste the bolt-shaped selection into the new document, and save it.

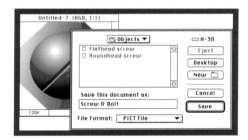

That's all for our metallic textures for now. Make sure you've made a gallery of textures from anything that sparked your interest from what we've created so far. They'll come in handy in your everyday work and in the chapters ahead.

Chapter 3

Creating Rocks and Gravel

One of the greatest features of Adobe Photoshop is its ability to create random patterns from which you can build natural-looking textures. In this chapter, you'll learn how to create wonderfully lifelike textures that resemble a variety of stones, gravels, rocks, and even stucco.

Best of all, you have ultimate control over the coarseness, depth, color, and type of all your natural textures. You learn how to use the Noise filter and channels to create some very effective textures and patterns. Then, you add an illusion of depth by layering effects on top of each other and give them any coloring you choose to create your own custom environments.

The techniques shown in this chapter are among the most powerful tools you learn from this work, yet they are simple to use and wonderfully effective.

Creating a Stucco Texture

Stucco is a great texture effect that's easy to create in Photoshop. Using simple tools, such as the Emboss filter, the Noise filter, and color, you can create different variations of roughness, texture, and hue. For this demonstration, you'll create three different levels of coarseness. Save these iterations of the stucco texture in your library of textures to use later in other illustrations.

To create the stucco texture, follow these steps:

Step 1.

Create a new document measuring 640 by 480 pixels in RGB Color mode, with a resolution of 72 pixels/inch.

Step 2.

You will apply this texture technique to the entire working area, so choose **All** from the **Select** menu (or press Command-A).

Step 3.

Choose **Add Noise** from the **Noise** submenu of the **Filter** menu to add some video static to the area. Set the amount to 999 to achieve the maximum effect. Choose Gaussian distribution.

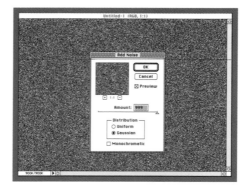

Step 4.

This is where you begin to determine how coarse the stucco effect will be. Choose **Gaussian Blur** from the **Blur** submenu of the **Filter** menu. Set the radius to 3 pixels.

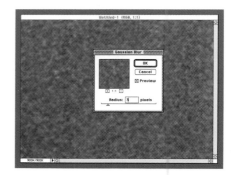

Setting a larger gaussian blur radius results in a coarser stucco pattern.

Step 5.

Choose **Hue/Saturation** from the **Adjust** submenu of the **Image** menu. Click the Preview check box only. Remove most of the range of color from your image.

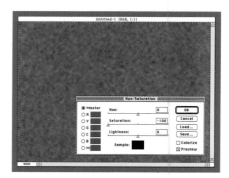

Stucco is a fairly "edgy" texture effect, but your current image has the appearance of gray dryer lint. Therefore, you must enhance the contrast of the image to create a harder-edged pattern.

Step 6.

Choose **Brightness/Contrast** from the **Adjust** submenu of the **Image** menu. Change the contrast value to 100 to remove all the shades of gray between white and black.

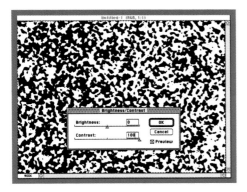

Now you're getting somewhere. Next, you need to add some dimension to the pattern you just created.

Step 7.

Choose **Emboss** from the **Stylize** submenu of the **Filter** menu to raise the edges of the pattern. Set the angle to 135° and the height to 1.

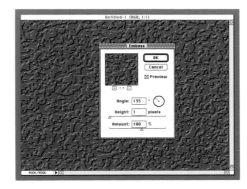

Step 8.

Add a little life to the effect. Choose **Blur More** from the **Blur** submenu of the **Filter** menu. This softens the edges of your pattern.

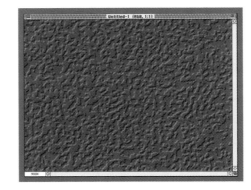

How about that? Your very own stucco texture, and without hiring a single interior decorator!

Step 9.

For the final touch, you should colorize your pattern. Choose **Hue/Saturation** from the **Adjust** submenu of the **Image** menu. Be sure the Colorize and Preview options are selected.

If you want to change the color of your stucco to a light flamingo pink, change the Hue value to 0, Saturation to 100, and Lightness to 80.

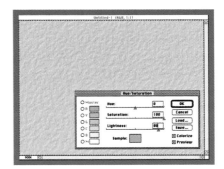

If you want to color your stucco a nice turquoise blue-green, change the Hue value to 180, Saturation to 50, and Lightness to -5.

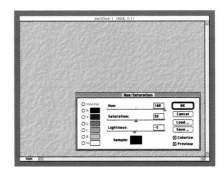

Save your favorite Stucco textures in your work folder to use later.

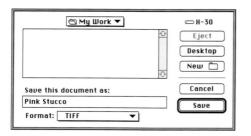

Finer Stucco Texture

You can create a finer stucco texture with a simple adjustment of the Gaussian Blur filter. Follow these steps:

Step 1.

Create a new document, measuring 640 by 480 pixels in RGB Color mode, with a resolution of 72 pixels/inch.

Step 2.

Choose **All** from the **Select** menu (or press Command-A).

Step 3.

Choose **Add Noise** from the **Noise** submenu of the **Filter** menu. Set the amount to 999.

Step 4.

Click **OK**.

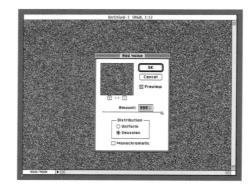

Step 5.

Choose **Gaussian Blur** from the **Blur** submenu of the **Filter** menu. This time, set the radius to 1 pixel.

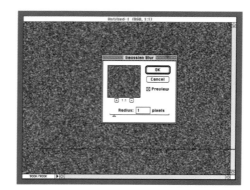

Step 6.

Next, remove the range of colors. Choose **Hue/Saturation** from the **Adjust** submenu of the **Image** menu. Click the Preview check box only. Set the Saturation value to -100.

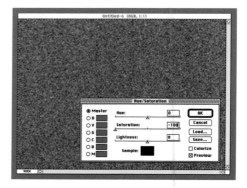

Step 7.

Choose **Brightness/Contrast** from the **Adjust** submenu of the **Image** menu. Boost the contrast all the way up, converting the entire range of grays to just black and white.

Step 8.

Choose **Emboss** from the **Stylize** submenu of the **Filter** menu. Set the angle to 135° and the height to 1.

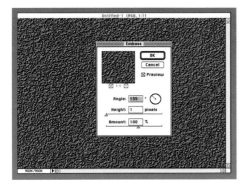

Step 9.

Choose **Blur More** from the **Blur** submenu of the **Filter** menu to soften it up a bit.

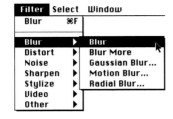

Step 10.

Choose **Brightness/Contrast** from the **Adjust** submenu of the **Image** menu. Adjust the sliders until you get an acceptable image.

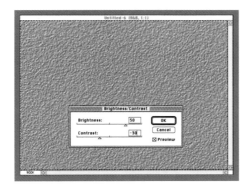

You may want to save this gray stucco texture to your library. Remember, you can always colorize the gray images to suit any scene.

Step 11.

Choose **Hue/Saturation** from the **Adjust** submenu of the **Image** menu to colorize the image. Try a few different color schemes to get the look you want.

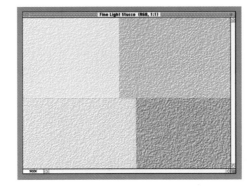

Coarser Stucco Texture

Now let's try a much coarser stucco texture. Follow these steps:

Step 1.

Create a new document measuring 640 by 480 pixels in RGB Color mode, with a resolution of 72 pixels/inch.

Step 2.

Choose **Add Noise** from the **Noise** submenu of the **Filter** menu to add the prerequisite video noise to the image.

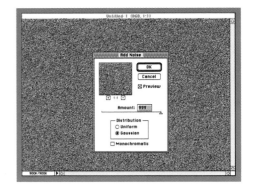

Step 3.

Choose **Gaussian Blur** from the **Blur** submenu of the **Filter** menu. Set the radius to 6 to really spread the pixels around.

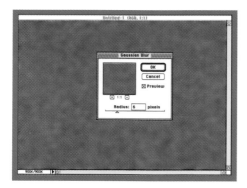

Step 4.

Choose **Hue/Saturation** from the **Adjust** submenu of the **Image** menu. Click the Preview check box only. Set the saturation to -100 to remove the color range.

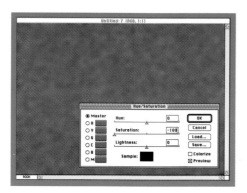

Step 5.

Choose **Brightness/Contrast** from the **Adjust** submenu of the **Image** menu. Set the contrast to 100 to make the image high-contrast.

Step 6.

Choose **Emboss** from the **Stylize** submenu of the **Filter** menu. Set the angle to 135° and the height to 1.

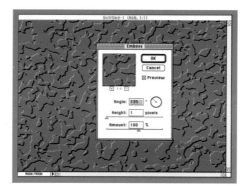

Step 7.

Finally, choose **Blur More** from the **Blur** submenu of the **Filter** menu to add a subtle softening to the texture.

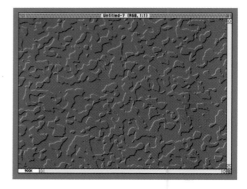

You may want to save the texture in your library for future use.

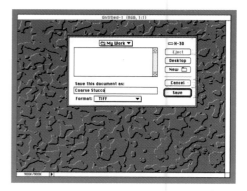

Stucco is a simple-to-execute technique that you can save and use over and over again!

Multi-Layer Stucco

The stucco texture effect, although dramatic enough, can be enhanced with a simple change in the order of the steps you use to create it. You can create a multiple-layer effect. It's an easy transition that involves most of the same steps used to create the original stucco texture. This time, you'll change the order of two of the steps and get a completely new stucco texture. Follow these steps:

Step 1.

Create a new document measuring 640 by 480 pixels in RGB Color mode, with a resolution of 72 pixels/inch.

Step 2.

Choose **All** from the **Select** menu (or press Command-A) to select the entire image.

Step 3.

Choose **Add Noise** from the **Noise** submenu of the **Filter** menu. Set the amount to 999 and click the Gaussian radio button.

Step 4.

Choose **Gaussian Blur** from the **Blur** submenu of the **Filter** menu. Set the radius to a comfortable limit. Assuming that you have tried a few different values in the previous section, you should have a feel for what will give you the best results.

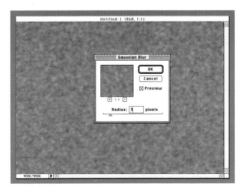

Step 5.

Choose **Brightness/Contrast** from the **Adjust** submenu of the **Image** menu. Set the contrast to 100 and leave the brightness at 0.

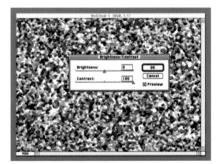

You can already see how there's more detail in the selection than in the previous effort.

Step 6.

Choose **Emboss** from the **Stylize** submenu of the **Filter** menu. Set the angle to 135° and the height to 1 to complete the embossed effect.

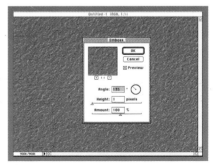

Step 7.

Choose **Hue/Saturation** from the **Adjust** submenu of the **Image** menu. Click the Preview check box only. Set the saturation value to -100 to remove all the color information in the selection.

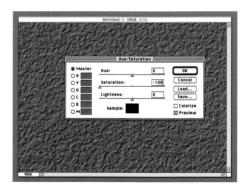

Step 8.

Finish the effect by adjusting the brightness and colorizing the texture any way you like.

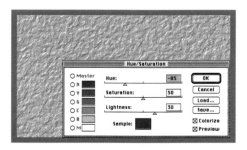

Save the texture to your library. This is much better than the basic stucco effect.

Remember, you can change the radius of the gaussian blur in step 4 to control the coarseness of the stucco texture.

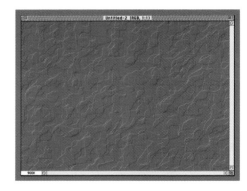

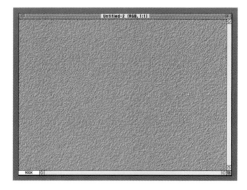

Creating Pink Marble Texture

Pink Marble is a nice texture that works great as a background or as an object texture. It gives a solid feel anywhere you apply it. You can alter it to appear smooth and shiny or coarse and rough by adding gradient blends or enhancing the contrast and brightness.

Follow these steps:

Step 1.

Create a new document measuring 640 by 480 pixels in RGB Color mode, with a resolution of 72 pixels/inch.

You need to start by laying down a good basis on which you will build the rest of the texture.

Step 2.

Choose **Add Noise** from the **Noise** submenu of the **Filter** menu. Set the amount to 999.

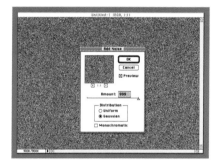

Step 3.

Choose **Gaussian Blur** from the **Blur** submenu of the **Filter** menu. Set the radius to 12 to really spread the pixels around in a mildly lumpy texture.

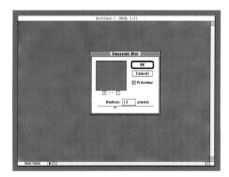

Step 4.

Choose **Hue/Saturation** from the **Adjust** submenu of the **Image** menu. Click the Colorize and Preview check boxes. Set the Hue value to 0, the Saturation to 50, and the Lightness to 40.

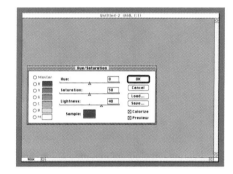

Note how you have done all this so far without selecting the image area. Because no selection is made, the filters are applied to the entire image area. Now you need to build onto the base texture by adding some detail.

Step 5.

Choose **Show Channels** from the **Window** menu to create a new channel.

Step 6.

In this new channel, add some random gaussian noise. Choose **Add Noise** from the **Noise** submenu of the **Filter** menu. Set the amount to 999.

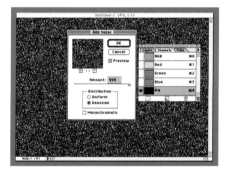

Remember, changes you make in additional channels will appear in grayscale only. Colors are visible in the RGB channel only.

Step 7.

Blur all the pixels in this channel. Choose **Gaussian Blur** from the **Blur** submenu of the **Filter** menu. Set the radius to 4 pixels.

Step 8.

Next you're going to make the texture more gritty and rough. Choose **Diffuse** from the **Stylize** submenu of the **Filter** menu to scatter the pixels about a bit. Set the mode to normal and reapply this filter about six times until you get a rough and random scattering of pixels.

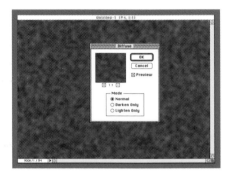

Step 9.

Now, you need to enhance the contrast a bit. This gives the texture harder edges, which are easier to select with the Magic Wand tool later. Choose **Brightness/Contrast** from the **Adjust** submenu of the **Image** menu (or press Command-B). Leave the Brightness at 0 and set the Contrast to 80.

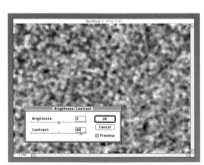

Step 10.

Choose **Emboss** from the **Stylize** submenu of the **Filter** menu. Set the angle to 135° and the height to 1 pixel for a relatively subtle effect.

Step 11.

Use the Magic Wand tool to select a medium gray area somewhere in the center of the image, then choose **Similar** from the **Select** menu to select all the other gray pixels in the image.

Step 12.

Return to the RGB channel. See how the selection is still active even though you have changed channels? The changes you make will affect the RGB pixels in this channel.

Step 13.

Choose **Feather** from the **Select** menu to create a transitional area around all the selected pixels. Set the feather radius to 1 pixel.

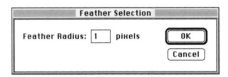

Step 14.

To get a clearer picture of the changes you make, choose **Hide Edges** from the **Select** menu.

Step 15.

Choose **Brightness/Contrast** from the **Adjust** submenu of the **Image** menu. Set the Brightness value to -30 to darken the selected pixels by about 30 percent.

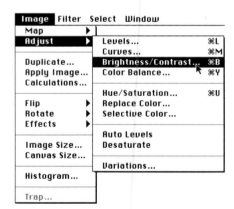

Step 16.

Next, add a bit of accent to the texture by making some pixels darker. Return to the extra channel. Use the Magic Wand tool to select just the darkest black pixels in the embossed texture. Choose **Similar** from the **Select** menu.

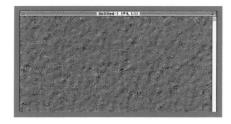

Tip: You can make it easier to select specific pixels by activating the Caps Lock key before using the Magic Wand tool. This changes the cursor from the Magic Wand cursor to a crosshair cursor.

Step 17.

Return to the RGB channel. You can do this by selecting Show Channels from the Window menu, or by the keyboard short-cut Command-0.

Step 18.

Choose **Feather** from the **Select** menu. Feather the selection by 1 pixel.

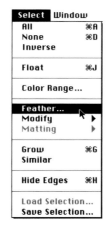

Step 19.

Choose **Hide Edges** from the **Select** menu to hide the selection.

Step 20.

Choose **Brightness/Contrast** from the **Adjust** submenu of the **Image** menu. Change the Brightness value to -100 to darken the selected pixels.

Step 21.

Choose **Brightness/Contrast** again. Darken the selected pixels even more.

Step 22.

Go back to the extra channel and select only the white pixels created by the emboss effect.

Step 23.

Use the Magic Wand tool to click on a white pixel, then choose **Similar** from the **Select** menu.

Step 24.

Choose **Feather** from the **Select** menu. Set the radius to 1 pixel and return to the RGB channel.

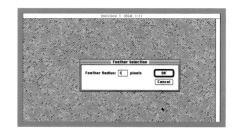

Step 25.

Choose **Brightness/Contrast** one more time. Lighten up the selection a bit.

If you want to add some lighter accents to the highlights, return to the extra channel, reselect the lighter pixels, and repeat the last step, leaving out the Feather command.

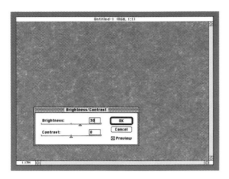

Voilà! Your own genuine Italian marble texture. This texture will make a great addition to your library collection.

Creating Rock Texture

In this section, you'll learn to create a wonderfully natural-looking rock texture. It's a great effect that you can apply to almost any setting. It's easy to create, it takes just a few simple steps, and every time you create this texture its random nature makes it entirely different from the last time.

You can control the roughness and character of the texture each time it's easily colorized, making it easy for you to custom-design any landscape. Follow these steps:

Step 1.

Create a new document measuring 640 by 480 pixels in RGB Color mode, with a resolution of 72 pixels/inch.

Step 2.

Next, add some random gaussian noise. Choose **Add Noise** from the **Noise** submenu of the **Filter** menu. Set the amount to 999.

Step 3.

Choose **Blur More** from the **Blur** submenu of the **Filter** menu. This blurs the noise into a more fuzzy dot pattern. Repeat this filter a few times to soften the effect a bit.

Step 4.

Now you have to add some rough edges to the blurred image. Choose **Diffuse** from the **Stylize** submenu of the **Filter** menu. Repeat this filter four or five times to splatter the pixels about a bit.

Step 5.

Choose **Hue/Saturation** from the **Adjust** submenu of the **Image** menu. Click both the Colorize and Preview check boxes. Set the Saturation value to -100 to remove all the color from the image.

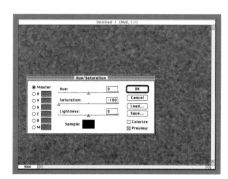

Step 6.

Now to make this a rough and rocky finish. Choose **Emboss** form the **Stylize** submenu of the **Filter** menu. Enter an angle of 135° and a height of 1 pixel.

Now that was easy, wasn't it? You can easily colorize the image if you want. Choose **Hue/Saturation** from the **Adjust** submenu of the **Filter** menu. Click both the Colorize and Preview check boxes and drag the sliders back and forth until you achieve the color you're looking for.

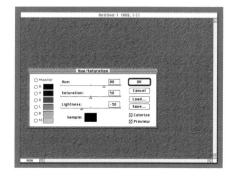

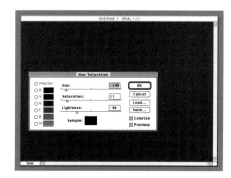

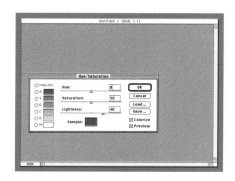

You can vary the sharpness and unevenness of the rock texture. Repeat steps 1 through 4 to create the base texture. (Apply the Diffuse filter a few more times if you want to spread the pixels around some more.) Choose **Brightness/Contrast** and change the contrast value to 80% to boost the division between the levels of gray tones in the texture. Now apply the same Emboss filter you just employed to finish the texture.

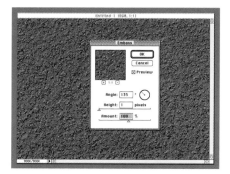

Another great way to add some variety to the generic rock texture is to apply a gaussian blur with a wider radius. Follow these steps:

Step 1.

Create a new document measuring 640 by 480 pixels in RGB Color mode, with a resolution of 72 pixels/inch.

Step 2.

Next, add some random gaussian noise. Choose **Add Noise** from the **Noise** submenu of the **Filter** menu. Set the amount to 999.

Step 3.

Choose **Gaussian Blur** from the **Blur** submenu of the **Filter** menu. Set the radius to 6 pixels.

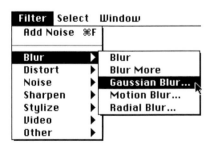

Step 4.

Choose **Diffuse** from the **Stylize** submenu the **Filter** menu. Repeat this filter six times.

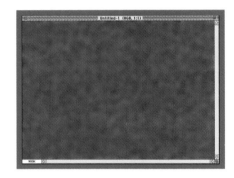

Step 5.

Now, condense the full range of colors to simple grayscales. Choose **Hue/Saturation** from the **Adjust** submenu of the **Image** menu.

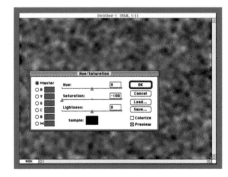

Change the saturation value to -100.

Step 6.

Now for a little visual prestidigitation. Choose **Brightness/Contrast** from the **Adjust** submenu of the **Image** menu. Set the contrast to 80%.

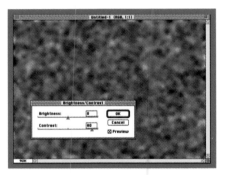

Step 7.

Repeat step 6 to really enhance the contrast.

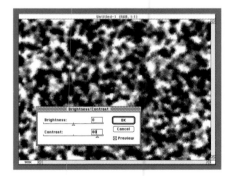

Step 8.

Choose **Emboss** from the **Stylize** submenu of the **Filter** menu. Enter an angle of 135° and make the height 1 pixel.

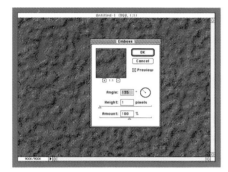

You can almost see the moss and lichen growing on the computer screen already.

You may want to save this texture to the working library for use later as a background texture. Saving the image as a grayscale texture enables you to apply color as needed to enhance any illustration.

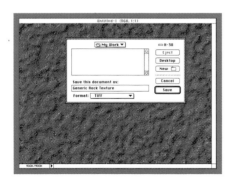

Creating Sandstone Texture

The technique for creating the sandstone texture is wonderfully effective. It looks very natural and uncannily real if performed properly.

First, you create a random noise texture, and then you emboss, colorize, and enhance it using simple filter steps. Then, you create natural-looking layers and striations by adding effects from another channel and mixing them together in the RGB channel.

This effect is bound to be one of your favorites. You will find plenty of uses for it as a background texture, but it also makes a great object texture for letter forms and type objects.

Follow these steps:

Step 1.

Create a new document measuring 640 by 480 pixels in RGB Color mode, with a resolution of 72 pixels/inch.

Step 2.

Choose **Add Noise** from the **Noise** submenu of the **Filter** menu. Set the amount to 999.

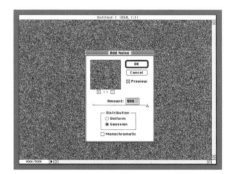

Step 3.

Choose **Emboss** from the **Stylize** submenu of the **Filter** menu.

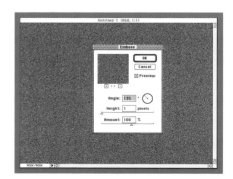

Set the angle to 135° and the height to 1 pixel. You want this texture to start out fairly grainy.

Step 4.

Now, add some color. Choose **Hue/Saturation** from the **Adjust** submenu of the **Image** menu. Make sure that the Colorize and Preview check boxes are clicked. Set the Hue value to 40, the Saturation to 50, and the Lightness to 20.

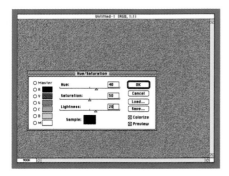

Step 5.

There, that's quick and easy, but a little grainy perhaps. Smooth it out by applying a simple blur filter. Choose **Blur More** from the **Blur** submenu of the **Filter** menu to apply a smooth blur to the entire image.

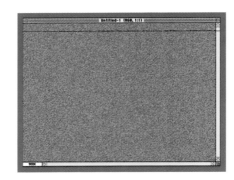

Reapply the blur filter to the image until you get the background texture that looks best to you.

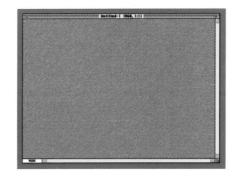

You can create an infinite variety of permutations of this effect simply by applying different Hue/Saturation filters to the image.

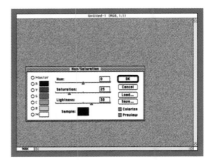

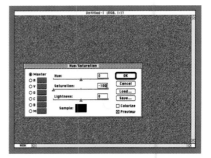

You can also adjust the contrast curves of the texture. Choose **Curves** from the **Adjust** submenu of the **Image** menu (or press Command-M). Experiment with manually adjusting the contrast curve.

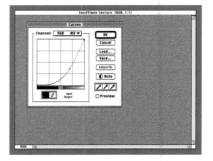

You can also try making a more finely detailed version of this image by selecting a portion of the image, reducing it in size and using that reduced selection as a pattern tile. To do this, complete the following steps:

Step 1.

Select a homogenous-looking section of the image using the Rectangular Marquee tool.

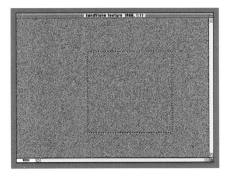

Step 2.

Choose **Scale** from the **Effects** submenu of the **Image** menu.

Step 3.

Hold down the Shift key as you drag one of the handles to create a smaller image area from the selection.

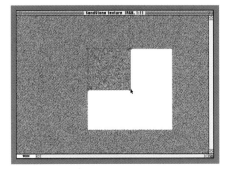

Step 4.

While the smaller area is still selected, choose **Define Pattern** from the **Edit** menu.

Step 5.

Choose **All** from the **Select** menu (or press Command-A) to select the entire image.

Step 6.

Choose **Fill** from the **Edit** menu. Choose Pattern from the pull-down menu to fill the entire image with the new pattern tile.

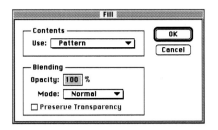

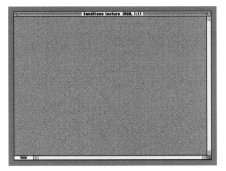

A pretty nice trick for smoothing out the graininess of the sandstone texture. Now you can also adjust the contrast and brightness to this new texture to change its character.

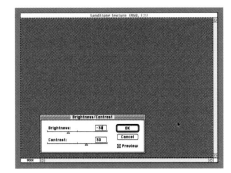

As you can see, it is easy to come up with thousands of different variations of this technique in a short time. It might be a good idea to save one basic version of this sandstone texture and then create the custom variations from the basic texture.

Creating Layered Sandstone

This section presents an interesting enhancement to the sandstone texture: sedimented or layered sandstone. Follow these steps:

Step 1.

Create a new document measuring 640 by 480 pixels in RGB Color mode, with a resolution of 72 pixels/inch.

Step 2.

Choose **Add Noise** from the **Noise** submenu of the **Filter** menu. Set the amount to 999.

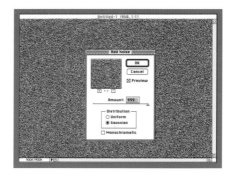

Step 3.

Choose **Motion Blur** from the **Blur** submenu of the **Filter** menu. Set the angle to 0° and the distance to 60 pixels.

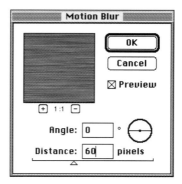

Step 4.

You will want the image without the streaks that appear at the sides of the image from the blur filter, so use the Rectangular Marquee tool to select a homogenous area within the texture.

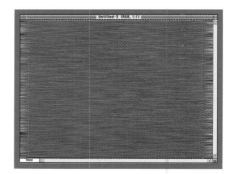

Step 5.

Choose **Crop** from the **Edit** menu to remove all the pixels outside of the selected area.

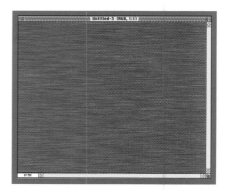

Step 6.

Choose **Show Channels** from the **Window** menu.

Step 7.

Choose **New Channel** from the palette's pop-up menu.

Step 8.

While you're in the new channel, choose **Add Noise** from the **Noise** submenu of the **Filter** menu. Set the amount to 999 and choose Gaussian distribution.

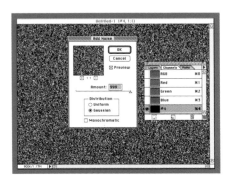

Remember, additional channels display your work in grayscale only. Everything eventually will end up in RGB Color mode, even though you're only seeing shades of gray now.

Step 9.

Choose **Blur More** from the **Blur** submenu of the **Filter** menu. Reapply this filter three or four times to spread pixels around.

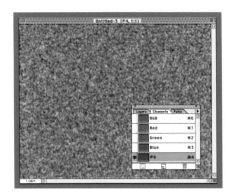

Step 10.

Choose **Diffuse** from the **Stylize** submenu of the **Filter** menu. Repeat this filter about six times to really rough up the image.

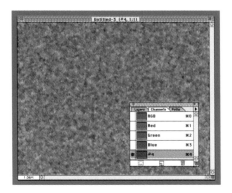

Step 11.

Choose **Brightness/Contrast** from the **Adjust** submenu of the **Image** menu (or press Command-B). Set the contrast to 80.

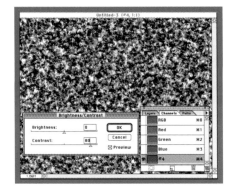

Step 12.

Choose **Emboss** from the **Stylize** submenu of the **Filter** menu to apply a simple emboss effect to the diffused noise texture in the new channel. Set the angle to 135° and the height to 1 pixel.

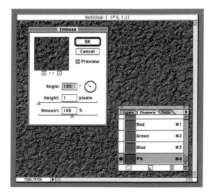

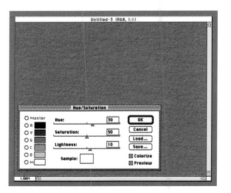

Step 13.

Choose **All** from the **Select** menu (or press Command-**A**).

Step 14.

Choose **Copy** from the **Edit** menu to make a copy of this channel on the clipboard.

Step 14.

Return to the RGB channel. Deselect the selection by choosing **None** from the **Select** menu (or by pressing Command-D).

Step 16.

Display the Layers palette by choosing **Show Layers** under the **Palettes** submenu of the **Window** menu. Now you can choose an opacity value for the floating selection. Set the opacity to 40% and the mode to Multiply to texturize the streaked background.

You can try several different color schemes on this texture:

Step 1.

Choose **All** from the **Select** menu (or press Command-**A**) to select everything (the background and foreground combined textures).

Step 2.

Choose **Hue/Saturation** from the **Adjust** submenu of the **Image** menu. Click the Preview and Colorize check boxes to add some color to the texture. Move the Hue slider back and forth to choose a general color, then move the Saturation and Lightness sliders to refine the color choice.

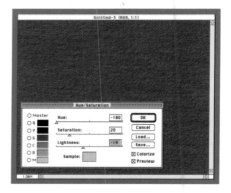

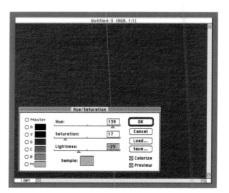

Wow! A definite candidate for the next Photoshop rendering. Don't forget to save this image into the working library.

You can subtly change the character of this texture technique by changing the intensity and pattern of the base streaks before pasting in the embossed texture. Try applying more contrast to the streaks, then applying some wave or ripple effects to the streaks before pasting the embossed texture over them.

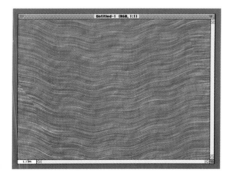

You might also try using a coarser embossed pattern over the streaks. You can do this by applying a fatter Gaussian blur before diffusing the random noise pattern in the extra channel.

Tip: Using a less saturated, lighter color makes a better background. It appears more subtle and natural looking.

*Creating a
Simple Tile
Pattern*

page 74

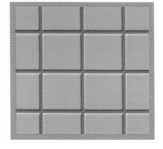

*Adding
Grout*

page 78

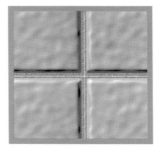

*Adding a
Smooth
Rippled Finish*

page 82

*Making a
Brick Pattern*

page 91

*Enhancing the
Brick Texture*

page 95

Chapter 4

Tiles and Bricks

In this chapter, you learn to create textures for tiles, bricks, and cobblestones. Photoshop has a built-in feature that automatically creates patterns. The trick to realistic-looking tiles and bricks is using that feature to create the repeating texture necessary for these textures.

Creating a Simple Tile Pattern

Let's start with a simple tile pattern to use as a wall, a backdrop for a scene, a texture for a floor, or just a simple ornament. Follow these steps:

Step 1.

Create a new document measuring 640 by 480 pixels in RGB color mode, with a resolution of 72 pixels/inch. Now you have a document window big enough for an object with plenty of space around it.

Step 2.

Create a perfectly square selection by holding down the Shift key while you drag diagonally with the Rectangular Marquee tool.

This is the basic shape you will use to create the first tile. Remember, your background pattern is basically a repeating shape that fills an area you select later. By making this original object a perfect square, you're ensuring that the pieces of the pattern will fit together seamlessly.

Step 3.

Choose **Fill** from the **Edit** menu. Select a medium green color for the foreground color and fill the area with the foreground color at 100% opacity.

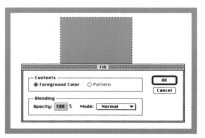

Step 4.

Now to give the tile a little depth and life. While the square selection is still selected, choose the Airbrush tool. Choose **Show Brushes** from the **Window** menu. Select a medium sized brush, set the brush pressure to 30%, and the mode to Darken.

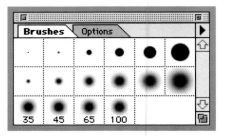

Step 5.

Set the foreground and background colors to black and white. (As a shortcut, you can click on the Default Colors icon in the lower left corner of the tool palette.)

Step 6.

Here's a great little Photoshop trick. Holding down the Shift key when you click with any of the painting tools paints a straight line between the origin point and the destination point. Whenever you paint within a selected area, the selection masks the background so that the paint actions apply only in the selection.

Using the Airbrush tool, click the lower left corner of the square selection.

Hold down the Shift key and click the lower right corner of the square selection.

Hold down the Shift key and click the top right corner of the square selection.

So far, so good. Let's complete the illusion of depth by creating a highlighted edge using white paint this time.

Step 7.

You must change the settings for your brushes palette. Keep the brush pressure at 30% and the brush size the same. But reverse the foreground and background colors to white and black (as a shortcut, you can click the Switch Colors icon) and change the mode to Lighten.

Now you need to do essentially the same steps in reverse for the highlights on the top and left edges of the square selection. Follow these steps:

Step 8.

Using the Airbrush tool, click the top right edge of the square selection.

Hold down the Shift key and click the top left edge of the square selection.

Hold down the Shift key and click the bottom left edge of the square selection.

Step 9.

Just for effect, click the top left corner of the selection again to create a little extra highlight, adding some life to the image.

Step 10.

It might not be a bad idea to save this image as a tile for later use. While it's still selected, from the **Edit** menu, choose **Copy**.

Step 11.

Choose **New** from the **File** menu to create a new document. You'll use this new document for pasting the Clipboard image.

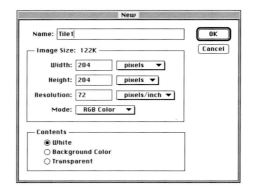

Tip: A great shortcut for this technique is to choose **Crop** from the **Edit** menu to reduce the document size to the size of the actual selection.

Save this new document as Tile1 in the working folder.

Trying Out the Effect

Let's experiment and try out the new tile as a pattern. Follow these steps:

Step 1.

While the selection is still active in the new document window (that you have titled Tile1), choose **Define Pattern** from the **Edit** menu. This copies the selection to the Clipboard as a pattern with which you can fill any other selection.

Step 2.

Return to the original document in which you created the tile. If it is still open, you can get there by choosing it from the **Window** menu, or by closing the smaller Tile1 window. Your original tile object will still be visible in the center of this working area, but that's OK. You will cover it up in a step or two.

Step 3.

Choose **All** from the **Select** menu to select the entire area of this window.

Step 4.

Here's the fun (and easy) part. While the selection is still active, choose **Fill** from the **Edit** menu and then choose Pattern from the pull-down menu.

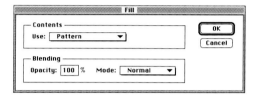

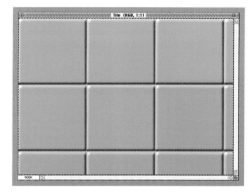

Here's how the document will look with the tiles filling the selection. Not bad, and an easy effect to achieve, but how about making the elements of the tile pattern smaller? To accomplish this, follow these steps:

Step 1.

The original tile you created should still be on the clipboard, ready to paste into the document. (If it's not, you can open the

Tile1 document, select it, and copy from there). Choose **Paste** from the **Edit** menu, to place the original tile selection into this working area.

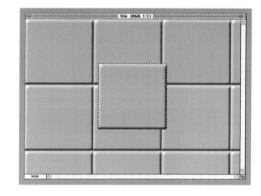

Step 2.

Now to resize the element and redefine it as a pattern tile. Choose **Scale** from the **Effects** submenu of the **Image** menu. Hold down the Shift key and drag the top right corner of the selection down and to the left to resize the selection.

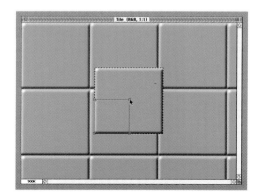

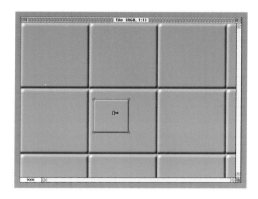

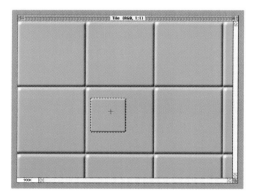

Step 3.

After reducing the scale of the image, click inside the selection to apply the effect.

Step 4.

While the newly reduced selection is still active, choose **Define Pattern** from the **Edit** menu to make this new, smaller tile the pattern element.

Step 5.

Choose **All** from the **Select** menu to select the entire working area.

Step 6.

Choose **Fill** from the **Edit** menu. Set the opacity to 100% and make sure that Pattern is selected from the pull-down menu.

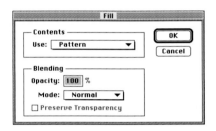

Here are the new, resized tiles.

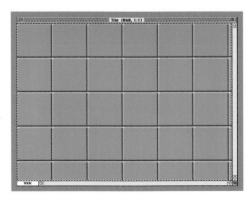

Adding Grout

Let's liven up this pattern by adding some grout between the tiles. Adding grout is easy enough. All you have to do is surround the tile object. But in any computer-related task, it makes sense to let the machine do all the work—it's much faster and more precise than you are. Follow these steps:

Step 1.

Create a new document measuring 640 by 480 pixels in RGB color mode with a resolution of 72 pixels/inch.

Step 2.

Open the Tile1 document that you created in the previous steps and copy it into the new document.

Step 3.

Next, you need to create a wide outline around the selection. Click once on the foreground color swatch and choose a nice midtone gray from the color picker.

Remember, this color has to be significantly different from the background and the tile itself. The Magic Wand tool, looks for differences in color density to find the edges of the selection it chooses.

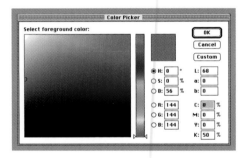

Step 4.

While the tile is still selected, choose **Stroke** from the **Edit** menu.

Step 5.

Apply a six-pixel stroke to the outside of the selection.

You can see how the stroke around the tile is beveled on the corners.

You will have to touch up those areas to make sure that the corners of the pattern all match perfectly. To do this, follow these steps:

Step 1.

Choose **None** from the **Select** menu (or press Command-D) to deselect the tile object.

Step 2.

From the tool palette, choose the Pencil tool. Because the foreground color is still the same gray you just created, you can use the Pencil tool to touch up the corners of the outside stroke.

Step 3.

You might want to work in a close-up view, editing the corners pixel by pixel. Press Command-spacebar to change over to the magnifying tool, then click on the area you want to magnify to see your work close up.

Now to create a new pattern. Follow these steps:

Step 1.

Using the Rectangular Marquee tool, select the new tile object (including the surrounding grout).

(As long as you have the tile and grout selected, now might be a good time to save the object as another document that you can come back to later. Choose **Copy** from the **Edit** menu and create a new document for pasting the Clipboard contents. Once again, Photoshop remembers the size of the selection and creates a new document with the same parameters.)

Step 2.

When this new object is selected, choose **Define Pattern** from the **Edit** menu. Now you're ready to apply this pattern to any selection.

Let's apply the new pattern to the open document.

Step 3.

Choose **All** from the **Select** menu to select the entire image area.

Step 4.

Choose **Fill** from the **Edit** menu. Make sure that Pattern is selected from the pull-down menu.

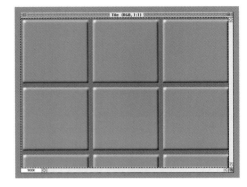

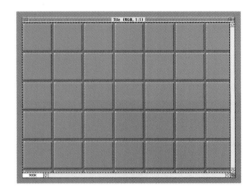

Adding Texture To Your Grout

You can add some life to your tile image by altering the look of the grout. In this section, you'll learn how to add some subtle texture to the grout. It only takes a few extra steps, but it really enhances the looks. Follow these steps:

Step 1.

Open a new document. Paste the tile with grout artwork into it.

Step 2.

Double-click the Magic Wand in the tool-bar. Change the Tolerance setting to 0 and disable anti-aliasing.

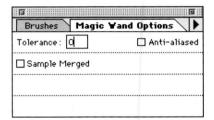

Step 3.

Using the Magic Wand tool, click once on the grout surrounding the tile. This selects only the grout.

Step 4.

Choose **Add Noise** from the **Noise** submenu of the **Filter** menu. Set the noise level to 32 and choose Gaussian to add just the right sprinkling of texture to the selection.

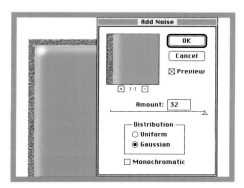

Step 5.

Choose **Emboss** from the **Stylize** submenu of the **Filter** menu. Set the angle to 135° and the height to 3 pixels.

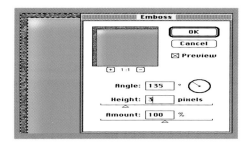

Step 6.

Pretty, but not quite there yet; you need to soften the effect. Choose **Blur More** from the **Blur** submenu of the **Filter** menu. Reapply the filter (using the keyboard shortcut **Command-F**) until you get the look you want.

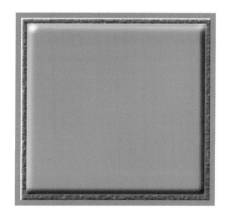

Step 7.

You can soften the effect even further by adjusting the brightness and contrast of the selection. Choose **Brightness/Contrast** from the **Adjust** submenu of the **Image** menu.

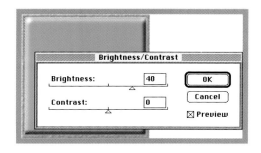

This is looking pretty good! Let's try it out as a pattern.

Step 8.

Use the Rectangular Marquee tool from the tool palette to select the tile and grout.

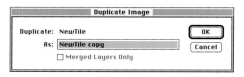

(Here's a good place to create a new document and save this new selection as another variation of the tile pattern. Choose **Copy** from the **Edit** menu. Choose **New** from the **File** menu for a new document. Paste the selection into the new document and save it for later use.)

Step 9.

Choose **Define Pattern** from the **Edit menu** to make this new selection a pattern.

Step 10.

Now to apply the pattern. Choose **All** from the **Select** menu to select the entire image.

Step 11.

Choose **Fill** from the **Edit** menu and select Pattern from the pull-down menu to fill the entire area with the new pattern.

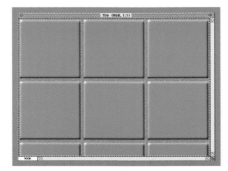

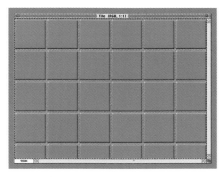

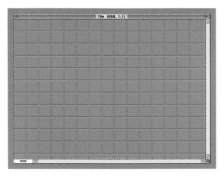

Adding a Smooth Rippled Finish to the Tile

In this section, you learn how to add a smooth rippled finish to the tile. This will give you a little more variety in the kind of tiles you create. Follow these steps:

Step 1.

Open the most recent tile you created. This should be the one with the textured grout.

Step 2.

Choose **Duplicate** from the **Calculate** sub-menu of the **Image** menu to create an exact duplicate of the original file.

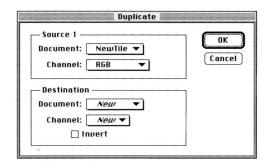

Step 3.

Use the Rectangular Marquee tool to select the tile area only (leaving out the surrounding grout texture).

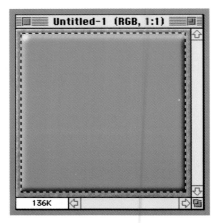

Step 4.

Choose **Copy** from the **Edit** menu to keep a copy of the selection on the Clipboard.

Step 5.

Create a new channel to do your next manipulation. Choose **Show Channels** from the **Windows** menu, and select **New Channel** from the palette's pop-up menu. Name it something descriptive like Ripple. This will match the title bar in the next image. Your selection is still active in the new channel.

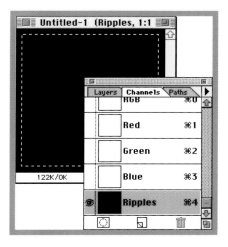

Step 6.

Choose **Add Noise** from the **Noise** sub-menu of the **Filter** menu.

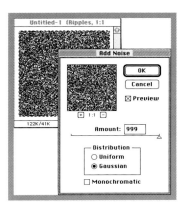

Step 7.

Choose **Gaussian Blur** from the **Blur** sub-menu of the **Filter** menu. Set the radius to 6 pixels.

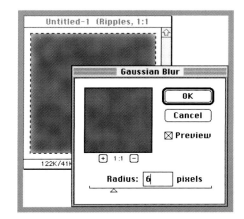

Step 8.

To enhance the contrast a bit, choose **Brightness/Contrast** from the **Adjust** sub-menu of the **Image** menu. Set the Brightness to 30 and the Contrast to 60.

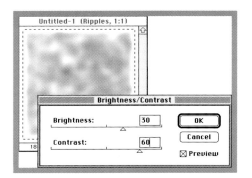

This is a nice effect in itself, but let's add some dimension to it.

Step 9.

Choose **Emboss** from the **Stylize** submenu of the **Filter** menu.

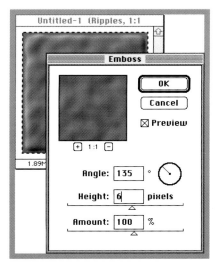

Set the depth to 6 pixels. This will give you a subtle texture to work with.

Tip: You could enhance this image even further using the Brightness and Contrast controls.

Step 10.

Now to add this wonderful texture to the RGB channel. While the rippled texture is still selected, choose **Copy** from the **Edit** menu to copy this selection to the Clipboard.

Step 11.

Go back to the RGB channel (keyboard shortcut is **Command-0**). Notice how the tile area is still selected, and all the work you just did in the other channel is not evident.

Step 12.

Return to the RGB channel and click the Layers tab in the Layers/Channels/Paths group to display your layers options palette.

Step 13.

Paste your rippled texture into the selected area and set your Mode to Lighten and your opacity to 100%.

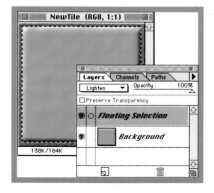

This isn't too remarkable; there's not very much contrast. It's almost too subtle.

Step 14.

Now paste your clipboard texture into your selection area again.

Step 15.

Choose Darken from the Mode pop-up menu and set the Opacity to 50% to keep most of the underlying image visible. This gives you some contrast to balance the image.

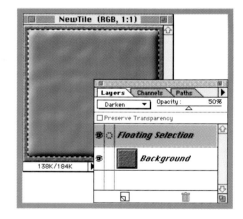

Step 16.

Click OK.

Almost there. Looks a little gray, doesn't it? That's easily enhanced by adjusting the brightness and contrast for the image.

Step 17.

Choose **Brightness/Contrast** from the **Adjust** submenu of the **Image** menu to change the contrast of the selection.

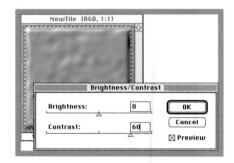

Ta-daaaa! Save this image as a new document in the project folder. Try it as a pattern for a new background.

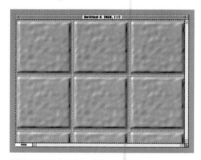

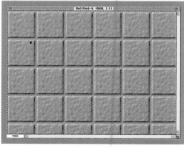

Creating a Brick Texture

You can probably imagine any number of possibilities for using tiles to create a regular, repeating background pattern. You can use the same technique to create a repeating brick pattern. It's just a bit more complex than regular square tiles, but the basic technique and practice are the same.

For this demonstration, you'll create a repeating brick pattern that looks lifelike, right down to the rough texture of the brick itself. Once you have created a single brick, you will see how easy it is to create a repeating and interlocking pattern.

Follow these steps:

Step 1.

Create a new document measuring 640 by 480 pixels in RGB color mode, with a resolution of 72 pixels/inch.

Step 2.

Double-click the Rectangular Marquee tool. This will allow you to set the size of your selection area.

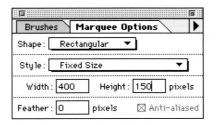

Step 3.

Click the Fixed Size radio button and set the horizontal value to 400 pixels and the vertical height to 150 pixels. (Constraining the size and shape of selections made with this tool makes it easier to select and create shapes identical to the original.)

Step 4.

Click the upper left quadrant of the working area to create a rectangular selection with the exact dimensions that you just defined.

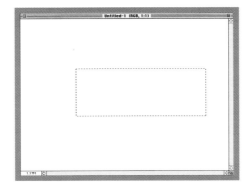

Step 5.

Next, you need to fill the selection with a suitable brick color. Click the foreground color swatch and choose a brick-red color from the options in the Color Picker dialog box.

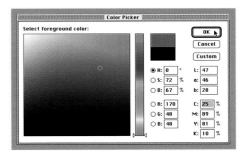

Step 6.

Choose **Fill** from the **Edit** menu and set the Opacity to 100%. Make sure that the Foreground option is selected.

Step 7.

Next, you need to make the background color a darker variation of the foreground. Hold down the Option key while you use the Eyedropper tool to click once on the interior of the selection. This makes the background color the same as the foreground.

Step 8.

Click the background color in the toolbox and add more black to the background color.

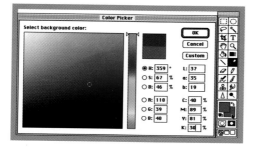

Step 9.

The brick shape is still selected. Choose the Gradient tool, then choose **Show Brushes** from the **Window** menu to display the brushes palette. Set the Opacity to 100%.

Step 10.

With the Gradient tool selected, click the image and drag diagonally across the length of the brick.

Step 11.

The next part of the process is to create a rough texture for the brick, which you do in another channel. Create a new channel and name it anything you want.

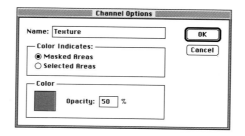

Step 12.

Your brick shape should still be selected in a clear area. Choose **Add Noise** from the **Noise** submenu of the **Filter** menu. Set the noise level to 32 and choose Gaussian distribution. Now choose **Invert** from the **Map** submenu of the **Image** menu. This will give you a light sprinkling of video noise to apply the next filter to.

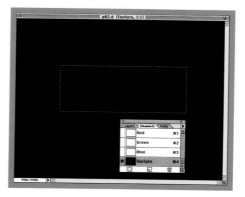

Step 13.

Choose **Emboss** from the **Stylize** submenu of the **Filter** menu. Set the angle to 135°, the height to 1 pixel, and the amount to 100% to give the selection a more subtle texture.

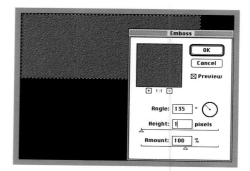

Step 14.

Repeat the filter to give the brick a nice kiln-baked look. Remember, you can always repeat a filter with Command-F.

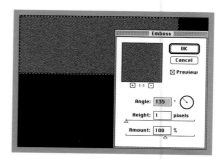

Step 15.

Choose **Blur More** from the **Blur** submenu of the **Filter** menu to soften the effect.

The next part of the process is to bring together the texture and the colored shape in the RGB channel. An easy way to do this is to copy the selection from the Texture channel into the RGB channel. Alternatively, you could spend some time experimenting with the various calculation commands from the Image menu to bring these two channels together. This demonstration uses the first method.

Step 16.

Choose **Copy** from the **Edit** menu.

Step 17.

Click on **RGB**, in the channel palette, which returns you to the RGB channel.

Step 18.

Hold down the Option key and choose **Paste** from the **Edit** menu (or press **Option-Command-V**). This automatically activates the Composite Controls, giving you control over the way you paste the texture into the selection.

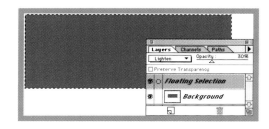

Step 19.

Set the Opacity to 30% and the mode to Lighten, and then click OK to add some subtle textural highlights to the brick color.

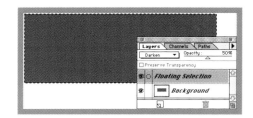

Step 20.

Press Option-Command-V to repeat this process. This time, set the Opacity to 50% and the mode to Darken to add some textural shadowing to the selection.

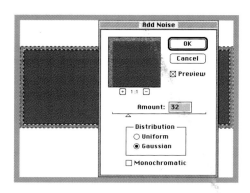

Adding Mortar

Remember how you added texture to the grout surrounding the tile? You can use the same technique to add a slightly rougher texture to the mortar surrounding your brick. Follow these steps:

Step 1.

To create a neutral color for the foreground, click the foreground color swatch in the tool palette.

Step 2.

Change the CMYK values to 0,0,0 and 50% to remove all but 50% of black, creating a neutral gray tone.

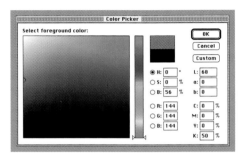

Step 3.

Choose **Stroke** from the **Edit** menu. Make the stroke 8 pixels wide, around the outside of the selection. This creates an outline around your brick shape to simulate mortar.

Step 4.

Next, you need to clean up the corners of the shape, making them perfectly square. This ensures that the edges of brick and mortar will all line up perfectly when you create your pattern. Choose **None** from the **Select** menu (or press Command-D) to deselect the selection.

Step 5.

Using the Magnifying tool, enlarge the view.

Step 6.

Using the Pencil tool, click each blank pixel to fill it in.

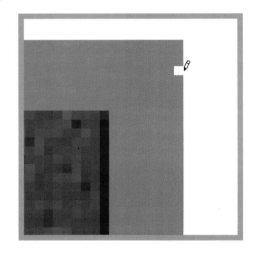

Step 7.

Using the Magic Wand tool, click the border to select the outside border.

Step 8.

Choose **Add Noise** from the **Noise** submenu of the **Filter** menu to add a little basic texture. Set the amount to 32 and choose Gaussian distribution.

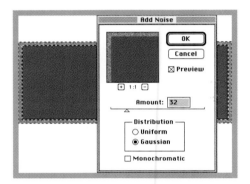

Step 9.

Choose **Emboss** from the **Stylize** submenu of the **Filter** menu to texturize the noise filter effect.

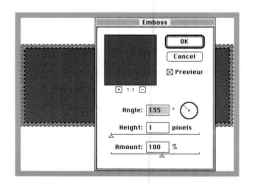

Step 10.

Choose **Blur More** from the **Blur** submenu of the **Filter** menu to soften the effect.

Step 11.

Choose **Brightness/Contrast** from the **Adjust** submenu of the **Image** menu. Lighten the color a bit.

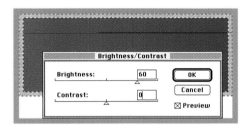

Adding Dimension

Aha! Now you're getting somewhere, but things still look a little flat.

In this section, you add some dimension using some offset selection techniques, then you add a few highlights manually. Follow these steps:

Step 1.

Return to the Texture channel and select the brick area.

Step 2.

If the Rectangular Marquee tool is still set to a Fixed Size, click the top left pixel in the selection. If not, double-click the tool and set your horizontal size to 400 pixels and your vertical size to 150 pixels.

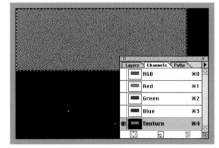

Next, you're going to use some special keyboard shortcuts to choose the bottom right and top left edges to apply shadows and highlights.

Step 3.

Hold down the Option and Command keys. Press the Left Arrow key four times and the Up Arrow key four times. This offsets the selection by four pixels.

Step 4.

With the Magic Wand tool selected, hold down the Shift key and click the background of the image. This isolates the desired selection area and adds the entire background to the current selection.

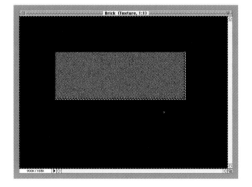

Notice how the area near the bottom right of the brick shape has been excluded.

Step 5.

Everything but the lower right corner of the brick is selected, but you want just that area selected. Choose **Inverse** from the **Select** menu.

Step 6.

Click RGB in the Channel palette to return to the RGB channel. The selected area is still active in this new channel.

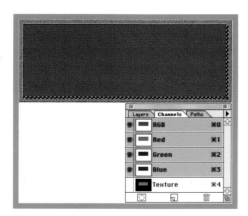

Step 7.

Choose **Feather** from the **Select** menu. Set the radius to 4 pixels.

Step 8.

Click the Default Colors icon in the lower left corner of the tool palette to set the foreground and background colors to black and white.

Step 9.

Choose **Fill** from the **Edit** menu. Set the Opacity to 60% and the mode to Darken to make the most of this effect.

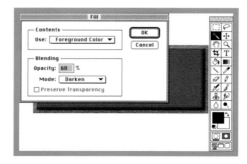

You may want to repeat this action a couple of times to get the exact level of contrast you want.

Step 10.

Select the textured area again.

Step 11.

Hold down the Option and Command keys. Press the Right Arrow key four times and the Down Arrow key four times to nudge the selection to the right and down by four pixels.

Step 12.

With the Magic Wand tool selected, hold down the Shift key and click the background area to add the background to the selection.

Step 13.

Choose **Inverse** from the **Select** menu to invert the selection.

Step 14.

Click RGB in the Channel palette to return to the RGB channel.

Step 15.

Choose **Feather** from the **Select** menu. Set the radius to 4 pixels.

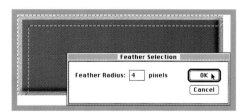

Step 16.

Click the Switch Colors icon to make the foreground color white.

Step 17.

Choose **Fill** from the **Edit** menu. Set the mode to Lighten and apply a 60% white fill.

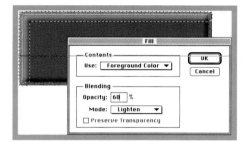

There, now. Isn't that much better?

Step 18.

You can add a little extra life by highlighting the top left corner of the brick. From the Brushes palette, choose a medium-sized brush and set the Opacity to 50%. Then click the top left corner of the brick.

Making a Brick Pattern

Earlier, you learned how to make a pattern using any selection. It's a little more complex with bricks, because the bricks in the pattern must interlock.

You must first select the brick and the surrounding mortar texture. If the Rectangular Marquee tool is still set to select a defined area, you will find this task a challenge.

The objective is to select all but the outside row of pixels of the brick to avoid selecting the darker outline pixels that were created when you embossed the mortar texture. You could double-click the Rectangular Marquee tool and then drag diagonally across the brick, but a more precise way is to alter the performance of the selection tool. Follow these steps:

Step 1.

Double-click the Rectangular Marquee tool to display the tool controls.

Step 2.

Change the Fixed Size setting to 414 by 164.

That's two pixels less than the total dimensions of the object. Remember that the 8-pixel border you made added 16 pixels to the overall dimensions of the original selection.

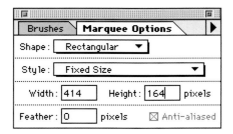

Step 3.

Click the top left corner of the art to select the brick and surrounding mortar.

Your Rectangular Marquee tool should select all but the outside border of pixels. If you need to adjust the selection's position, you can either click the top left corner again until you get the position correct, or you can press Option-Command and use the arrow keys to nudge the selection area one pixel at a time into position.

Step 4.

Choose **Copy** from the **Edit** menu to copy the selection to the Clipboard.

Step 5.

Now would be a good time to create a new document and paste the brick selection into the new document, saving it for later use.

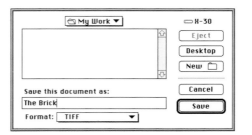

Step 6.

To demonstrate the difficulty of defining an interlocking staggered pattern, while the selection is still active choose **Define Pattern** from the **Edit** menu.

Step 7.

Choose **All** from the **Select** menu to select the entire working area.

Step 8.

Choose **Fill** from the **Edit** menu and choose Pattern from the pull-down menu to fill the area with the selected pattern design.

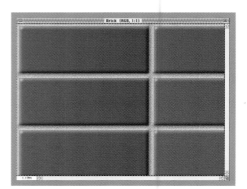

Of course, this isn't how bricks ordinarily appear, but it's a good way to see whether you have selected the bricks correctly. The division between the pattern tiles is pretty seamless; if you had selected the brick and mortar including the outside (darker) pixels originally, there would be a line separating the pattern tiles.

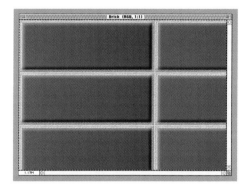

Step 9.

Select the Lasso tool, click in the selected area, and drag the brick down to move it to the lower half of the window so that you will have room to duplicate it.

Tip: You can constrain the movement to the horizontal or vertical axes by holding down the Shift key while you drag the selection.

Step 10.

While the Lasso tool is still selected, hold down the Option key and drag the selection up and to the left of its current position. (Holding down the Option key while you drag a selection automatically creates a clone of the selection).

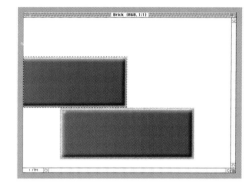

The ideal position for the second brick is halfway along the length of the original brick. In other words, the right edge of the surrounding mortar texture should be exactly in the middle of the original brick. (If you have trouble positioning the brick correctly, you can use a temporary positioning tool, as discussed in Chapter 1, *Wood Textures.*)

Step 11.

Finish the pattern by making another clone of the current selection. Hold down the Shift and Option keys and drag the selection horizontally until the left edge of the selection meets the right edge of the upper brick.

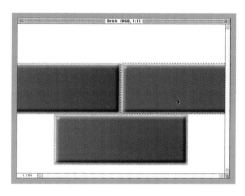

You now have all you need now to create an interlocking brick pattern.

Step 12.

Select the Rectangular Marquee tool and disable the Fixed Size option (if you still have that enabled).

Step 13.

Use the Rectangular Marquee tool to select the area shown below:

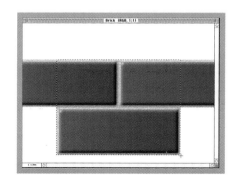

Step 14.

Choose **Copy** from the **Edit** menu and create a new document in which to store this.

You can also make a duplicate of the document; choose **Duplicate** from the **Calculate** submenu of the **Image** menu.

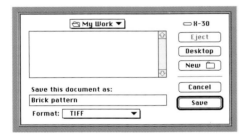

Name this copy Brick Pattern so that you can retrieve it later as needed.

Now you can experiment to see how this pattern measures up. Follow these steps:

Step 1.

While the selection is still active, Choose **Define Pattern** from the **Edit** menu.

Step 2.

Choose **All** from the **Select** menu.

Step 3.

Choose **Fill** from the **Edit** menu. Make sure that Pattern is selected from the pull-down menu. Set the opacity to 100% opacity and the mode to normal.

Step 4.

Click OK.

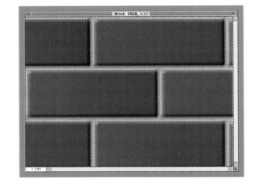

How would the bricks look if you made them smaller? Follow these steps:

Step 1.

Press the Delete key.

Step 2.

Paste a copy of the pattern (which should still be in the clipboard) into the working area.

Step 3.

Choose **Scale** from the **Effects** submenu of the **Image** menu.

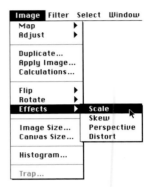

Step 4.

Hold down the Shift key to constrain the proportions of the selection as you drag one of the handles diagonally to reduce the selection's size.

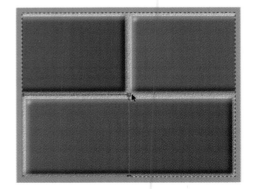

Step 5.

Click the center of the selection to apply the effect.

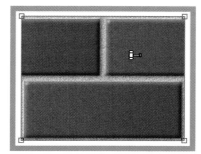

Step 6.

Choose **Define Pattern** from the **Edit** menu.

Step 7.

Choose **All** from the **Select** menu.

Step 8.

Choose **Fill** from the **Edit** menu to fill the selected area with the brick pattern.

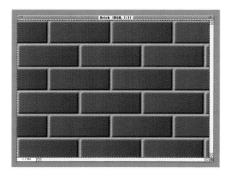

Enhancing the Brick Texture

You can enhance the texture by applying a few variations. Follow these steps to create a rougher texture for the basic brick:

Step 1.

Open the saved Brick image.

Step 2.

Select just the red interior area (remember, you can do this easily by setting the Rectangular Marquee tool to a fixed size).

Step 3.

Create a new channel to hold the texture.

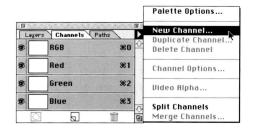

Step 4.

In the new channel, choose **Add Noise** from the **Noise** submenu of the **Filter** menu. Set the amount to 128.

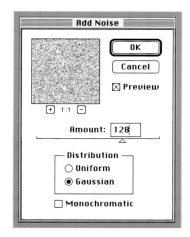

Step 5.

Choose **Gaussian Blur** from the **Blur** submenu of the **Filter** menu to blur the selection. Set the blur radius to 2 pixels.

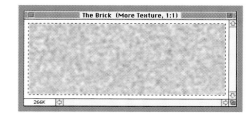

Step 6.

Choose **Emboss** from the **Stylize** submenu of the **Filter** menu. Set the angle to 135° and the depth to 6 pixels.

Step 7.

Choose **Brightness/Contrast** from the **Adjust** submenu of the **Image** menu. Set the brightness to 10 and the contrast value to 80 to enhance the contrast. This exaggerates the effect.

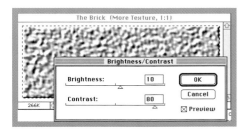

Now this is texture!

Step 8.

Choose **Copy** from the **Edit** menu.

Step 9.

Return to the RGB channel. Notice that the brick area is still selected in the RGB channel.

Step 10.

Paste your selection into the selected area in the RGB channel, then click the Layers tab in the Layers/Channels/Paths group palette to display your layers options. Set the opacity to 30% and the mode to Darken.

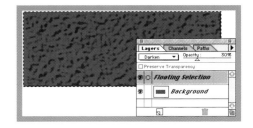

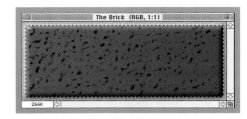

This gives a nice mottled effect.

Step 11.

Now repeat the same paste process, but this time set your mode to Lighten and the opacity to 60% by changing the settings in your Layers/Channels/Paths group palette.

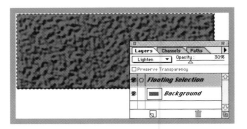

Step 12.

Choose **Curves** from the **Adjust** submenu of the **Image** menu.

Step 13.

You can manually adjust the curve to enhance the contrast curve of the image.

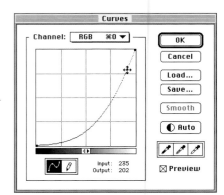

Step 14.

You can soften the effect of the curve's adjustment. Choose **Blur More** from the **Blur** submenu of the **Filter** menu.

Step 15.

Repeat this filter by pressing Command-F a few times to soften the effect to your taste.

Step 16.

If you want save this pattern, choose **Save As** from the **File** menu.

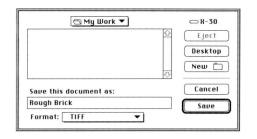

If you want, you can create a new brick pattern using this texture.

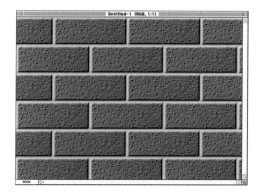

Remember, you can also add a gradient tint to the pattern background, just as you did with the tile backgrounds.

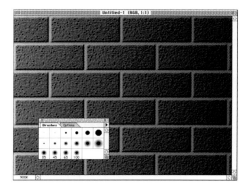

That's all there is to creating a very sophisticated brick background. Don't forget to save anything that you might want to use later. One of the best parts of computer-assisted design is that you never have to redraw anything.

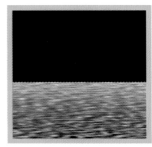

Chapter 5

Creating Environments

Photoshop lets you create wonderful landscape and environment images to use as backdrops and reflections in your objects, adding a dimension of realism and life to your renderings.

The trick is in maintaining a steady hand when working with colors. The Photoshop palette can manage over 16 million colors, so the challenge is in resisting the temptation of using the wildest, brightest colors in the palette. Subtle and sublime is the true road to nirvana.

Creating a Background

Let's start by learning a few quick tricks for creating a picturesque background. Follow these steps:

Step 1.

Create a new document measuring 640 by 480 pixels in RGB Color mode, with a resolution of 72 pixels/inch.

Step 2.

Using the Pencil tool or a fine brush and a solid black foreground color, draw a rough and random horizon line.

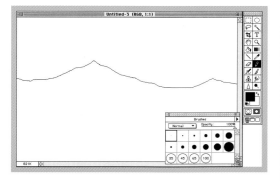

Make sure that the line you draw is continuous (with no breaks in the pixels) and connects both edges of the window.

If there are breaks in the line, the selection will spill up into the sky area, when you select the area in the lower half of the image.

Step 3.

Select the Magic Wand tool, then click the Wand options tab in the Brushes/Options palette. Set the tolerance level to 1 and disable anti-aliasing.

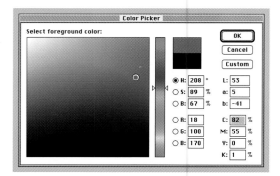

Step 4.

Click the bottom half of the image to select all the contiguous pixels.

Choose **Fill** from the **Edit** menu to fill the area with the foreground color.

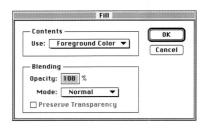

This creates a high-contrast, easily selectable area that you can play with later, after you create a nice graduated sky.

Step 5.

Time to create a crystal-clear summer sunset sky. Click the foreground color swatch in the Tool palette and select a rich sky blue. Click the background color swatch in the Tool palette and select a bright sunset color.

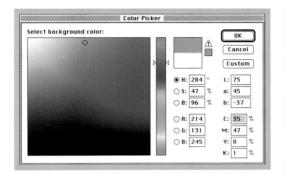

Note: If you're planning to produce this image as a four-color process reproduction, then make sure that you have chosen a color that will reproduce correctly. If the color will not reproduce accurately, Photoshop warns you by showing the warning symbol next to the color selection.

Step 6.

Next, fill the sky with graduated color. Using the Magic Wand tool, select the entire sky area. Set the tolerance level to 1 and disable anti-aliasing.

Step 7.

Choose the **Gradient** tool and drag the cursor vertically from the top of the selected area to the bottom.

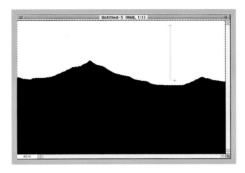

You can constrain the graduation to a perfect vertical gradation by holding the Shift key down while you drag the cursor.

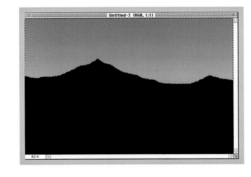

Note: To see more accurately where to add the fill effect, hide the selection marquee (the "marching ants") by choosing **Hide Edges** from the **Select** menu.

Now you have a pretty dramatic sunset started. You can make it even more picturesque by creating a reflecting body of water in the foreground, perhaps a still pond or shallow stream.

Step 8.

Using the Lasso tool, draw a stream-shape receding into the center of the image. This will become a selection that you can fill easily with the Gradient tool.

You can add non-contiguous areas to the selection by holding down the Shift key as you select different areas with the Lasso tool.

Tip: Before going on, you can change the selection to a path and save it using the Paths palette. This will give you instant access to the selected area whenever you want to come back to it, making the reselection process much easier.

To do this, click the Paths tab of the Layers/Channels/Paths group palette and choose Make Path from the pop-up menu that appears when you click the tiny triangle at the top right corner of this palette.

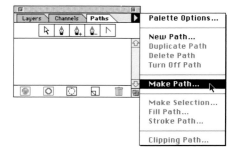

You can save this path and assign it a name so that you can reselect it later. You will have the option to adjust the tolerance of the path, that is, how closely the path will follow the edges of the selected pixels; set your value to 1 to retain details. Later, if you may want to create a selection from this path, choose Make Selection from the same pop-up menu.

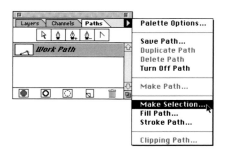

Step 9.

Your stream is a reflection of the sky, so you need to fill it with a reverse of the sky's graduation.

If you still have the same two colors selected in the foreground and background swatches, you can switch them by clicking the Switch Colors icon in the tool palette.

Note: If you don't have the sky's colors selected in the swatch area, it's easy to retrieve them by using the Eyedropper tool. Click at the points where you began and ended your gradation.

Just click the color your want for the foreground color, then hold down the Option key and click on the background color.

Step 10.

Select the Gradient tool, then choose **Show Brushes** from the **Window** menu to display the Brushes palette. Set the mode to Normal and the Opacity to 100%.

Step 11.

Using the Gradient tool, fill the selected area by dragging the tool vertically from the center to the bottom of the image.

Experiment with the graduation by trying a few different origin and destination points with the drag action. As long as the area is selected, you can fill and refill the area as often as you like.
Pretty dramatic effect, and simple to do. So far so good, right? Let's add another subtle effect to give it just one more touch of life.

Step 12.

Use the Magic Wand tool to select the foreground area (excluding the stream).

Step 13.

Choose two different foreground and background colors to use as a graduation for the background. Make them pretty close in color range so that the contrast will be subtle across the area.

Step 14.

Using the Gradient tool, drag vertically downwards across the area to add another level of subtlety to the image.

See how the subtle color change between the foreground and background of the image creates a subtle indication of depth and realism? Now for the final touch, a small ripple in the water.

Step 15.

Using the Elliptical Marquee tool, select a small part of the water area in the foreground. Try to keep the selection within the edges of the stream.

Step 16.

Choose **Distort** from the **Filter** menu, and then select **ZigZag**, turning the selection into a rippling river.

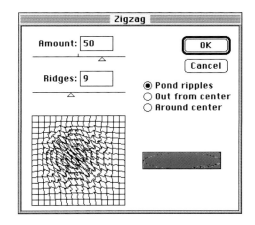

Tip: You can view a thumbnail of any dynamic filter effect by holding down the Option key while choosing "About Photoshop" under the Apple menu.

Step 17.

Add finishing touches such as clouds, grasses, and textures where appropriate.

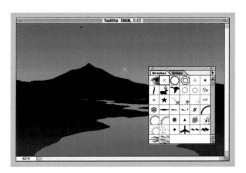

You can put a lone twilight star in the sky using one of the custom brushes supplied with Photoshop. You can also add a pebbled texture to the foreground by using the noise filter on a widely feathered selection in the foreground. Make the effect very subtle by choosing a low value in the Noise dialog box.

Voilà! A simple-to-create but dramatic natural background scene to use whenever you want. Now might be a good time to save this background for future use.

Creating a Serene Lake

Here's another natural scenery technique that you can apply as a background or reflected environment to any image. It's a variant of the reflected sky technique with a unique twist to give it a more natural look. Follow these steps:

Step 1.

Create another new document. measuring 640 by 480 pixels in RGB Color mode, with a resolution of 72 pixels/inch.

Step 2.

Using the Rectangular Marquee tool, select just the upper half of the image area.

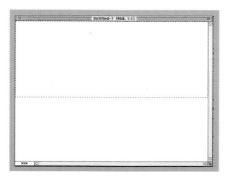

Step 3.

Click once on the foreground color swatch to display the Color Picker dialog box. Move the indicator sliders on either side of the Color Slide to a nice clear-blue travel-brochure azure hue, and then click in an area inside of the Color Field to choose the color.

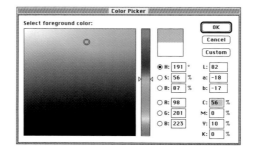

Beware the warning symbol (an exclamation point inside a triangle) that may appear when you choose a color. This indicates that you have chosen a color that cannot be reproduced because it does not have a CMYK equivalent. If you intend for the work to be reproducible using a CMYK production process, choose a color near the selection that doesn't produce the warning symbol, or click the warning symbol to have it select a similar color for you. Remember, you can always override the selection by clicking somewhere else in the palette area.

Step 4.

Click OK.

Step 5.

Double-click the Gradient tool and set the fill to a linear gradation. Click OK. Then, drag vertically from top to bottom across the selection area to fill it.

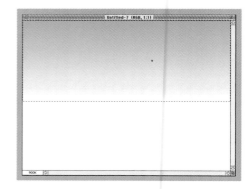

This is a nice sky so far. Let's add a distant and somewhat indistinct mountain range.

Step 6.

Deselect the sky area.

Step 7.

Using the Lasso tool, click and drag a nice mountain shape across the horizon.

Step 8.

When you get to the opposite side of the image area, hold down the Option key and release the mouse button while you move the cursor across the screen. This enables the cursor to travel across the image while still creating a straight-edged line to the selection.

Step 9.

Move the cursor across the image to the original side, click at the edge of the image area and release the Option key. When you release the mouse button, the selection automatically closes itself by joining the points where you pressed and then released the mouse button.

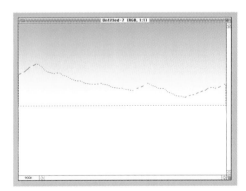

You need to apply a graduated color across the mountain range, simulating some depth and distance.

Step 10.

Click once on the foreground color swatch. In the Color Picker dialog box, move the indicator sliders to choose a nice dark color for your mountain. Click inside the Color Field to choose the color. Click OK.

Click once on the background color swatch and choose a lighter color for the background.

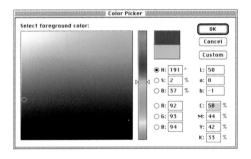

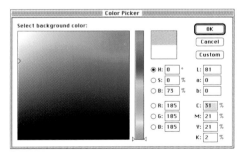

Step 11.

Using the Gradient tool, drag across the mountainous selection, top to bottom.

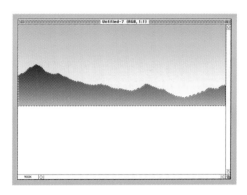

Now for some foreground detail.

Step 12.

Deselect the mountain shape.

Step 13.

Using the Lasso tool, create a wide, flat shape with a straight horizontal bottom boundary. This is a stand of trees in the distance.

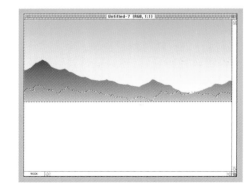

Step 14.

Choose **Add Noise** from the **Noise** submenu of the **Filter** menu to fill this area with some random noise. Experiment with different values.

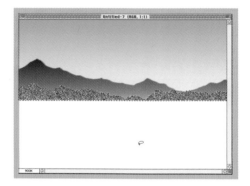

Step 15.

Choose **Blur More** from the **Blur** submenu of the **Filter** menu.

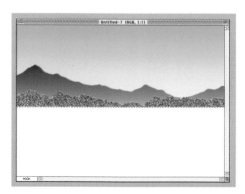

Step 16.

Next, you color the selection. Choose **Hue/Saturation** from the **Adjust** submenu of the **Image** menu. Make sure that the Colorize and Preview boxes are checked. Set the Hue value to 80, the Saturation to 100, and the Lightness to -70.

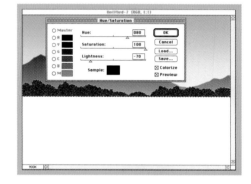

This will give the stand of trees a nice dark forest mottling. Next, you need to add some depth to the trees.

Step 17.

Hold down the Option key while you drag the tree shape. This makes a clone of the original selection. Move the clone down just enough so that you can still see some of the original trees behind the clone.

Step 18.

Choose **Horizontal** from the **Flip** submenu of the **Image** menu.

Step 19.

While the second layer of trees (the clone) is still selected, choose **Hue/Saturation** from the **Adjust** submenu of the **Image** menu. Make sure that the Preview and Colorize boxes are checked. Set the Hue value to 80, the Saturation to 90, and the Lightness to 0. This lightens the clone trees a bit.

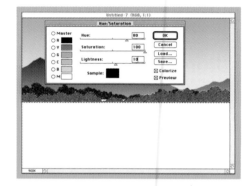

You could just as easily choose **Brightness/Contrast** from the **Adjust** submenu of the **Image** menu to achieve similar effects. Using the Hue/Saturation command, however, gives you more control over the color range of the selection.
So far, so good. Let's add a strip of beach sand across the base of the tree stand.

Step 20.

Use the Lasso tool to select a very wide area of sandy beach across the division between the trees and the horizon.

Step 21.

Next, you need to add a sandy texture. Choose **Add Noise** from the **Noise** submenu of the **Filter** menu. Keep the same values for the noise filter as before.

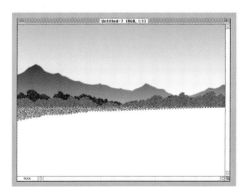

Step 22.

Choose **Blur** from the **Blur** submenu of the **Filter** menu to spread the pixels around.

Step 23.

Choose **Motion Blur** from the **Blur** submenu of the **Filter** menu. Set the angle to 0° and the distance to 10 pixels.

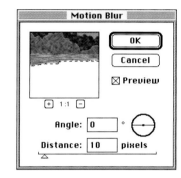

Step 24.

Choose **Hue/Saturation** from the **Adjust** submenu of the **Image** menu. Click the Colorize and Preview checkboxes and set the Hue value to 40, the Saturation to 60, and the Lightness to 20.

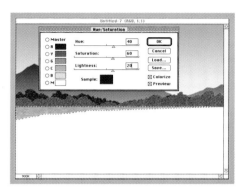

Step 25.

Use the Magic Wand tool to select all the white pixels at the bottom of the image.

Step 26.

Choose **Inverse** from the **Select** menu to select all the pixels except the white ones.

Step 27.

Choose **Copy** from the **Edit** menu.

Step 28.

Choose **Inverse** from the **Select** menu again to reselect the white pixels at the bottom of the image area.

Step 29.

Choose **Paste Into** from the **Edit** menu to paste the image on the clipboard into the selected area.

Step 30.

Choose **Vertical** from the **Flip** submenu of the **Image** menu to place a mirror image of the background into the selected area.

Step 31.

To move the selection into the correct position, just click and drag it into position.

Step 32.

You can add some life to the image. Choose **Motion Blur** from the **Blur** submenu of the **Filter** menu. Set the angle to 90° and the distance to 30 pixels.

Finally, you can apply a subtle distort filter to the selection to simulate ripples and waves to the water area.

Step 33.

Double-click the Magic Wand tool and set the tolerance to 64. This enables it to select a broader range of tonal variations.

Step 34.

Select most of the water area using the Magic Wand tool.

Step 35.

Choose **Feather** from the **Select** menu. Set the feather radius to 12 pixels to make a smooth transition between the filter you apply in the next step and the background image.

Step 36.

Choose **Zig Zag** from the **Distort** submenu of the the **Filter** menu.

You can try several different distortion filters to achieve your favorite wave and ripple effects. This is so real, you almost want to live there.

This technique is a great addition to your library of background images. Save it into your working library folder. Images like these are great for subtle backgrounds that show through windows or are reflected in shiny objects.

Creating a Lunar Landscape

In this section, you'll learn how to create a great homemade lunar landscape. Not everyone will have frequent need for lunar landscape textures; however, the trick applies equally well to natural environments (with a little modification) to create sand dunes, beaches, and underwater terrain. Follow these steps:

Step 1.

Create a new document measuring 640 by 480 pixels in RGB Color mode, with a resolution of 72 pixels/inch.

This exercise uses the channel capability to create an extra working area in which you can store some elements before placing them into the documents.

Step 2.

Create a new channel for this document. Begin by choosing **Show Channels** from the **Window** menu.

Step 3.

Click the triangle at the top-right corner of the palette. A pop-up menu appears.

Step 4.

Use the Rectangular Marquee tool to select the upper half of the image area.

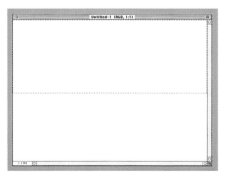

Make sure that the foreground and background colors are set to black and white.

Step 5.

Choose **Fill** from the **Edit** menu. Set the Opacity to 100% and the mode to Normal.

Now to create the tone and texture of the lunar foreground.

Step 6.

Select a small vertical area at the bottom-left corner of the image area.

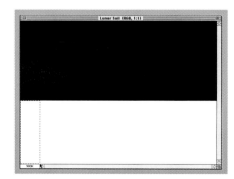

Step 7.

Choose **Add Noise** from the **Noise** submenu of the **Filter** menu. Set the amount to 999 and the distribution to Gaussian for maximum effect.

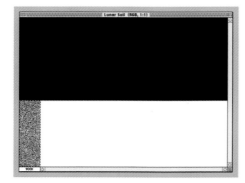

Step 8.

Choose **Blur More** from the **Blur** submenu of the **Filter** menu to spread the random noise pixels in the selected area.

Notice that the Filter menu's first item is now **Blur More**. Photoshop always remembers the last filter used and allows you to reapply the same filter by using the Command-F keyboard shortcut. Press Command-F now to apply the Blur More filter again.

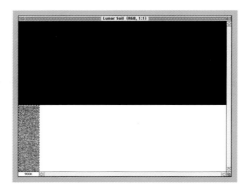

Step 9.

Choose **Emboss** from the **Stylize** submenu of the **Filter** menu. Set the angle to 135°, the height to 3 pixels, and the amount to 100%. This creates a pretty rough texture, but the next step will smooth this out considerably.

Step 10.

Choose **Scale** from the **Effects** submenu of the **Image** menu.

Step 11.

Click one of the corner handles on the right side of the selection to stretch the selection horizontally all the way across the image.

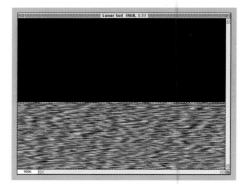

Pretty colorful for the surface of the moon. Next, change the color saturation to make it a gray lunar landscape.

Step 12.

Choose **Hue/Saturation** from the **Adjust** submenu of the **Image** menu. Make sure that only the Preview checkbox is clicked. Change the Saturation value to -100 by dragging the tiny triangle pointer under that slider all the way to the left.

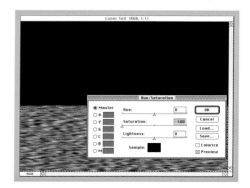

Wow! This looks just like the original photos sent back by the Pioneer lunar probes. You might want to leave the illustration just like this, but you can add a little bit of life to the rendering by shading selections.

Step 13.

Make sure that the crater area is still selected, and then select the Gradient tool from the tool palette.

Step 14.

Choose **Show Brushes**.from the **Window** menu. Set the Opacity to 50% and set the mode to Lighten.

Step 15.

Click the Switch Colors icon next to the color swatches in the Tool palette to change the foreground color to white. Drag the cursor vertically from the top of the selected area to the bottom. See how

the selection gradually lightens from the background forward?

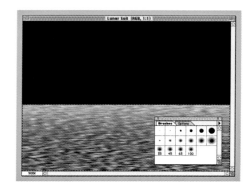

This makes for a great (albeit flat) lunar plain to which you can add illustrative objects. You can add a little variety to the horizon by drawing in some lunar hills and craters.

Step 16.

Let's save this backdrop for later use. Name it something like "Lunar Plain."

Step 17.

Choose **Duplicate** from the **Calculate** submenu of the **Image** menu to make a new copy on which to work for the next section.

Enhancing the Background with Hills

Creating hills is easy. Let's use the Path tools to create a perfectly smooth, round hill in the distance.

Step 1.

Choose **Show Paths** from the **Window** menu.

Step 2.

Select the Pen tool and click once on the horizon line near the center of the image.

Step 3.

Hold down the Shift key and click at the far left edge of the image. Using the Shift key this way constrains the creation of the path to a perfectly horizontal (or vertical) path.

Step 4.

Then, still holding down the Shift key, click a short way up on the left edge of the image.

Step 5.

Finish the hill by holding down the Option key while you click and drag away from the origin point.

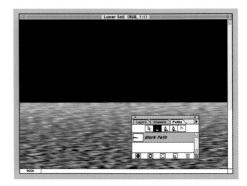

Step 6.

For safekeeping, save this path. Click the triangle in the upper right corner of the Paths palette. Choose Save Path from the pop-up menu that appears.

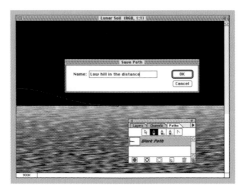

Step 7.

Repeat the same process in reverse, creating a slightly smaller hill against the right side of the image. Save that path as well. If the first path is still selected in the Paths palette, the new path will be included as part of the original path.

Next, you need to change these paths to selections and add some local color.

Step 8.

Make sure that the paths you just created are selected in the Paths palette (you will see their outline on-screen if they are), then click the Paths palette. Choose **Make Selection** from the pop-up menu that appears.

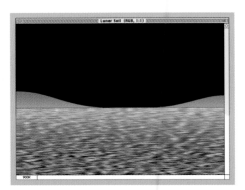

It would look too flat to just add a gray tone to the hill selection, so let's add some texture.

Step 9.

Choose **Add Noise** from the **Noise** submenu of the **Filter** menu to add a medium level of random pixels to the selection.

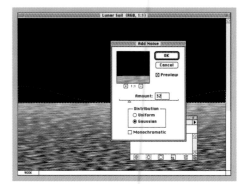

Step 10.

Choose **Blur More** from the **Blur** submenu of the **Filter** menu to spread the pixels around a bit. The image shouldn't change much on-screen. The next step makes the efforts more visible.

Step 11.

Choose **Emboss** from the **Stylize** submenu of the **Filter** menu to add a lumpy embossed texture to the selection.

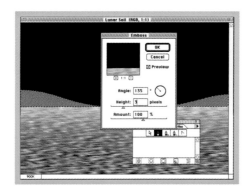

A nice effect, but let's enhance it by adding some graduated tone and adjusting the brightness to get it just right. You should choose two new foreground/background colors that are consistent with the colors found in the foreground.

Step 12.

To do this, use the eyedropper tool and click on a lighter color in the textured foreground. To choose a background color, repeat the process while holding down the Option key.

Step 13.

With the Gradient tool selected, choose **Show Brushes** from the **Palettes** submenu of the **Windows** menu, and set the Opacity to 50%.

Step 14.

Drag the cursor vertically upwards across the selection using the Gradient tool. This creates the illusion of moving the background farther away.

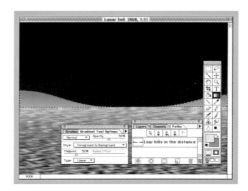

Drag the Gradient tool across the selection.

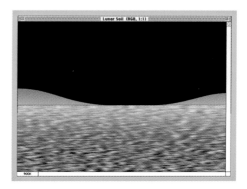

When you're working in RGB color mode, you'll notice some colored speckles in the gray tones of the textures in the hills. You remove them the same way you removed the rainbow colors from the landscape in the previous exercise.

Step 15.

Choose **Hue/Saturation** from the **Adjust** submenu of the **Image** menu. Do not click the Colorize checkbox. Reduce the Saturation value to -100 to remove all the color.

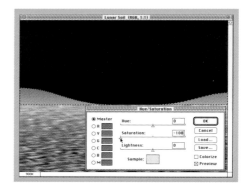

Now to blend the transition between the hills and the plain.

Step 16.

Using the Rectangular Marquee tool, select a few rows of pixels between the hills and the horizon line.

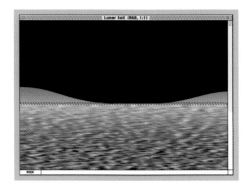

Step 17.

Choose **Feather** from the **Select** menu. Set the feather radius to 1 pixel.

Step 18.

Choose **Fill** from the **Edit** menu. Set the Opacity to 50% for a more natural transition. This fills the area with the light gray foreground color.

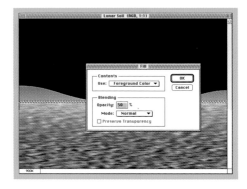

Step 19.

If you want, choose **Blur More** from the **Blur** submenu of the **Filter** menu to enhance the effect. Remember, you can use the Command-F keyboard shortcut to reapply the same filter.

You might want to save this as a reference image to come back to later. Save it as Lunar Hills in the same folder as the Lunar Plain image.

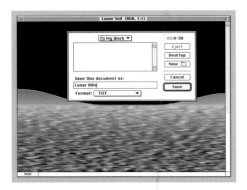

Changing Your Locale

In this section are a few quick tips for changing the location from the Moon to Mars or the bottom of the Caribbean. Let's first travel to the vacation planet Mars. Follow these steps:

Step 1.

Open the Lunar Hills illustration, making sure that the Mode menu choice is RGB color.

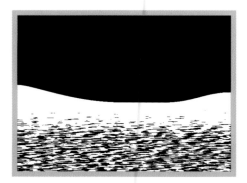

Step 2.

Choose **Duplicate** from the **Calculate** submenu of the **Image** menu to create a new copy of the illustration. You may want to save the new copy as Mars.

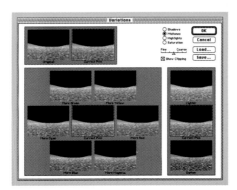

Step 3.

Choose **Variations** from the **Adjust** submenu of the **Image** menu.

Step 4.

Select the More Red option from the Variations window.

You can see how selecting More Red alters all the other options, relative to the current selection. Don't be shy about making broad and radical changes in this window. You can always change the selection back to where you started by clicking on the Original thumbnail.

You can enhance this simple adjustment. Choose **Color Balance** from the **Adjust** submenu of the **Image** menu. Do this to change the levels of the individual color channels precisely.

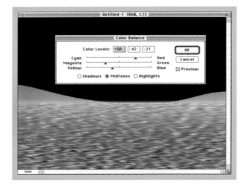

Changing Night to Day

You can now take your background and completely change the world you've created from night to day. Follow these steps:

Step 1.

Click the foreground color swatch in the tool palette.

Step 2.

Change the CMYK values to 0 to make the foreground color white.

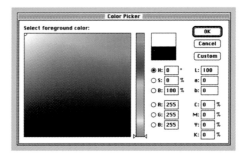

Step 3.

Hold down the Option key while using the Eyedropper tool to click on a selection in the textured foreground. Make the background color a light, dusky, lavender-pink. If you hold down the mouse button while you drag the Eyedropper tool around, you will see the background color swatch change as you move the cursor, picking up whatever color happens to be under the point of the eyedropper.

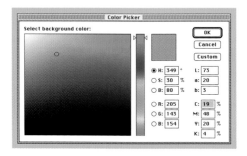

Now you have two complementary foreground and background colors to use in creating a graduated sky.

Step 4.

Using the Magic Wand tool, click once in the sky to select the sky area.

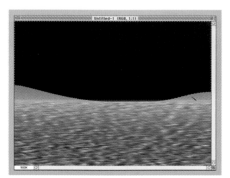

Step 5.

Now that the sky is selected, you can apply a gradient fill to it by selecting the Gradient tool in the tool palette and dragging across the selection. You can achieve two subtly different effects with the gradient tool by choosing a linear or radial gradation. You can change the style of gradation by double-clicking the Gradient tool and clicking either the Linear or Radial radio button. While the sky is still selected, try applying both styles of graduation to the background.

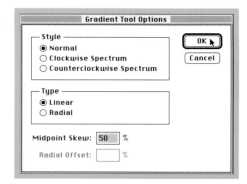

Tip: Make sure that the Brushes palette has the Opacity set to 100% to completely paint over the selection.

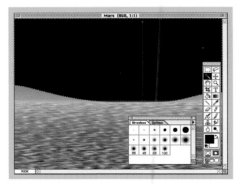

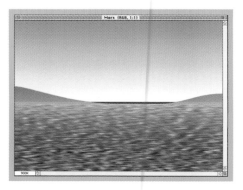

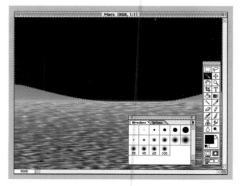

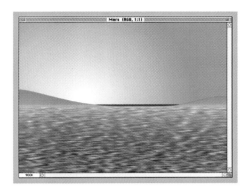

Welcome to Mars! For your safety and the safety of the passengers around you, the captain reminds you to please wait until the spacecraft has come to a complete stop before unbuckling the safety harness and standing up in the cabin. Save this document, call it Mars, and return here as often as you like to daydream.

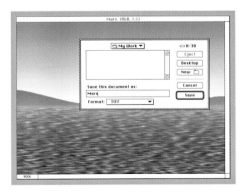

You can probably guess that the same technique you used to change the gray landscape to red can as easily be used to change the landscape to aquamarine blue for a fine ocean floor.

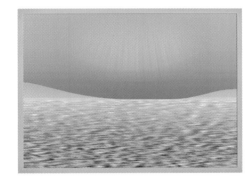

Making Your Own Foreground Trees

You can use the filters and paint tools in Photoshop to make natural-looking trees to add lifelike ornamentation to the illustrations.

You start by creating a simple two-dimensional silhouette, and then build on the technique to create wonderful looking three-dimensional foliage that you can save in the object library to place into any Photoshop document. Follow these steps:

Step 1.

Create a new document measuring 640 by 480 pixels in RGB color mode, with a resolution of 72 pixels/inch.

Step 2.

Use the Elliptical Marquee tool to select a vertical oval area that you will use as a very basic starter shape.

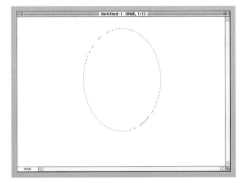

Step 3.

Choose **Add Noise** from the **Noise** submenu of the **Filter** menu to add some random noise for a nice coarse texture. Set the amount to 999 and choose Gaussian distribution.

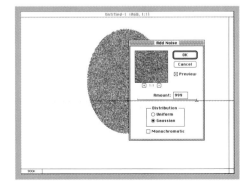

Step 4.

Eventually this will be a fairly coarse leafy texture, so you need to blur the noise. Choose **Blur More** from the **Blur** submenu of the **Filter** menu.

Step 5.

Now to create the leaves. Choose **Hue/ Saturation** from the **Adjust** submenu of the **Image** menu (or press Command-U). Make sure that only the Preview checkbox is clicked. Set the Saturation value to -100 to remove all the color variation in the selection.

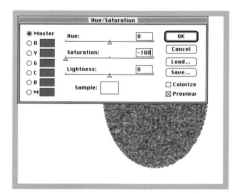

Step 6.

Choose **Brightness/Contrast** from the **Adjust** submenu of the **Image** menu. Move the Brightness slider all the way to the right, or enter a value of 100.

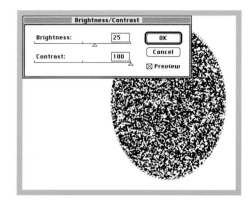

You may want to play around with the Brightness and Contrast sliders to get just the right level of random texture. Later, you use the Magic Wand tool to select the similar texture areas. You don't want the texture to be too thick, because the tool will select the entire shape (including its too-regular outside border), and you don't want the texture too sparse because the tool will not be able to select enough texture to work with.

Step 7.

Double-click the Magic Wand tool to define the threshold of shades that the tool will select. Make the setting 1 to constrain the selection to adjacent like-colored pixels, and check Anti-aliased to keep a small level of randomness in the selection.

Step 8.

Click OK.

Step 9.

Because the oval-shaped area is still active (you can see the selection marquee still marching around the ellipse), you need to deselect the area. Choose **None** from the **Select** menu or press Command-D.

Step 10.

Using the Magic Wand tool, click a solid black area near the center of the texture. There are two potential shortcomings of the selection technique. Look carefully at the general shape of the area the Magic Wand has selected. The selection may include the entire elliptical shape, which makes the selection too regular and artificial-looking; or the selection may be too sparse, which doesn't give you enough leaves to work with.

If the Magic Wand selected the entire elliptical area, try repeating the previous steps. Set the Brightness and Contrast to make a more sparse texture, and then reselect with the Magic Wand tool to get the shape you want.

If the selection appears too sparse, try selecting additional areas of the texture by holding down the Shift key while you click on alternate areas using the Magic Wand tool. (Alternatively, you may want to try choosing Grow from the Select menu to automatically add to the selection area.)

After you have selected an appealing and natural-looking area with the Magic Wand tool, you need to isolate the selection and remove everything else in the image.

Step 11.

Choose **Inverse** from the **Select** menu and then press the Delete key to remove everything except the selected texture.

Step 12.

Reselect the texture area. Choose **Inverse** from the **Select** menu again.

Choose **Brightness/Contrast** from the **Adjust** submenu of the **Image** menu. Set the Brightness to 0 and the contrast to 100.

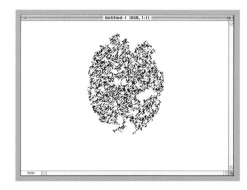

Note: Because of the random nature of the filter and select process, the image on the screen may not match those shown in this section.

As you can see, this is a great way to create and select nice, natural-looking, leafy textures. Next, you need to add the trunk and branches to the illustration.

Step 13.

Deselect everything by choosing **None** from the **Select** menu, or by using the Lasso tool and clicking anywhere outside of the leaves.

The Lasso tool can be a great drawing tool. Because you're creating a simple two-

dimensional silhouette of a tree, you can draw the trunk and branches right over the existing artwork.

Step 14.

Select the Lasso tool and drag it around the image in the shape of a tree trunk and branches. You can be as precise or as loose as you like with this to get the effect and shape that looks best to you.

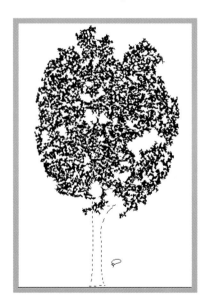

Step 15.

Set the foreground/background colors to black and white. Choose **Fill** from the **Edit** menu. Set the Opacity to 100%, matching the solid black of the leaves.

Step 16.

You can touch up the illustration by using the Lasso tool to select other parts of the leaves and clone them, pasting them over the solid trunk areas to make the image even more natural looking.

Clone an area here...

and paste over the solid trunk here to give the tree a more natural look

You can also use the other paint tools, such as the pencil or a small paintbrush, to add branches and leaves here and there. Be a digital tree-surgeon and sculpt the foliage any way you like.

Step 17.

Use the Magic Wand tool to select an area within the tree.

Tip: It's easiest to click on the trunk. Not all of the tree may be selected this time around. To make sure that you get the entire object, choose **Similar** from the **Select** menu. This selects all the pixels on the image that have the same tonal value as the currently selected area.

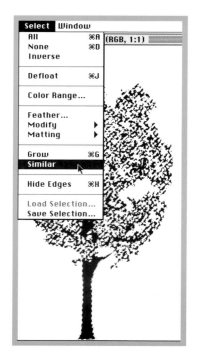

Step 18.

Choose **Copy** from the **Edit** menu to make a copy of the selection on the clipboard.

Step 19.

Choose **New** from the **File** menu to create a new document.
Paste the contents of the Clipboard into the new document.

Step 20.

Save the new document in the working file or object library to use later.

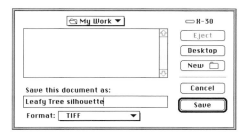

Try making a whole library of tree shapes that you can store and use often. One of the great features of this technique is that the simple one-color two-dimensional silhouette can be easily selected using the Magic Wand tool and the Similar command from the Select menu, and then pasted over any background you create.

It's especially effective when used with a darker sunset type picture.

Creating Colorful 3-Dimensional Trees

Now that you have learned the basics of creating simple tree silhouettes, here's a simple technique to make them colorful and three-dimensional.

Step 1.

Create a new document, measuring 640 by 480 pixels in RGB color mode, with a resolution of 72 pixels/inch.

Step 2.

The basis for this technique is very similar to the one you have just finished. Start with a basic tree shape like before. This time, try using the Lasso tool to define your own tree shape.

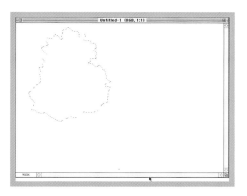

Make it small enough to allow you plenty of space to create and work with multiple copies of the shape.

Step 3.

Choose **Add Noise** from the **Noise** sub-menu of the **Filter** menu to fill the selected area with random Gaussian noise. Set the amount to 999 and choose Gaussian distribution.

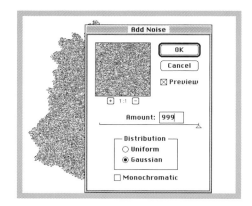

Step 4.

Choose **Blur More** from the **Blur** submenu of the **Filter** menu to blur the selection a bit. You can vary the coarseness of the leaf pattern in this step by creating a more blurry effect. Press Command-F to reapply the Blur More filter. Experiment a few times to get a feel for the final effect this creates.

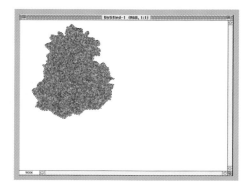

Step 5.

Choose **Hue/Saturation** from the **Adjust** submenu of the **Image** menu. Do not click the Colorize checkbox. Set the Saturation value to -100 to flatten out the range of colors to shades of gray.

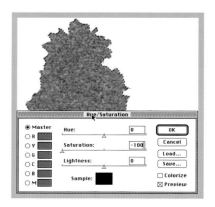

Step 6.

Let's take a moment to create a kind of subtool to help facilitate the process by which you make the layers. Choose **Copy** from the **Edit** menu (or press Command-C). Choose **New** from the **File** menu (or press Command-N). Choose **Paste** from the **Edit** menu (or press Command-V) to create a duplicate version of the image you have just started. Repeat this process two more times to create three new documents.

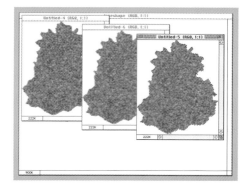

The advantage to making three new documents and tiling them on the screen is that you will be able to see all versions of the work simultaneously without making several new channels in the original document.

Step 7.

You want to create a leaf pattern in each new document, each with a varying level of contrast and brightness. Choose **Brightness/Contrast** from the **Adjust** submenu of the **Image** menu.

Step 8.

For the first document, which will be the bottom-most layer of the image, set the Brightness to 0 and the Contrast to 100. Make sure that the selection area is still active. This creates a good, solid base with just enough speckling to simulate light shining through the leaves in a few places.

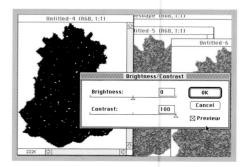

Step 9.

Next, activate the second window by clicking once on it. Make sure that the selection area is still active and, choose **Brightness/Contrast** from the **Adjust** submenu of the **Image** menu. Set the Brightness to 30 and the Contrast to 100.

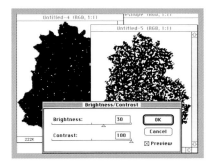

Step 10.

Finally, activate the third window, by clicking once on it. Make sure that the selection area inside is still active and, from the **Image** menu, choose **Adjust**, and then select **Brightness/Contrast**. Set the Brightness to 60 and the Contrast to 100.

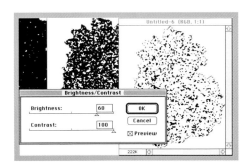

Now to colorize the tree layers. Start by colorizing and texturizing the bottom-most layer, because you will be pasting each successive layer from the bottom up.

Step 11.

Using the Magic Wand tool, click once on the black area. To make sure that you have selected everything you need, choose **Similar** from the **Select** menu.

Step 12.

Choose **Hue/Saturation** from the **Adjust** submenu of the **Image** menu. Make sure that the Colorize and Preview checkboxes are clicked. Set the Hue value to 80, the Saturation to 100, and the Lightness to 10.

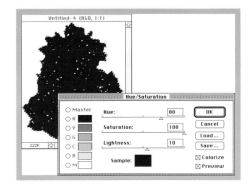

Step 13.

Activate the middle layer window, the one with a medium speckling texture, and repeat the process. Select the solid black areas by using the Magic Wand tool and

the Similar command from the Select menu.

Step 14.

Then, choose **Hue/Saturation** from the **Adjust** submenu of the **Image** menu (or press Command-U). Again, make sure that the Colorize and Preview check boxes are clicked.

Set the Hue to 80, and the Saturation to 100, and the Lightness to 20.

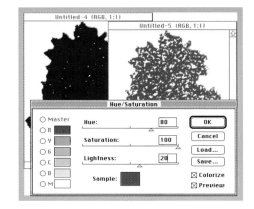

Step 15.

Finally, activate the top-most layer window, the one with the sparsest leaf texture, and repeat the same steps. Set the Hue to 80, the Saturation to 100, and the Lightness to 80 to create the light, leafy highlights for the tree.

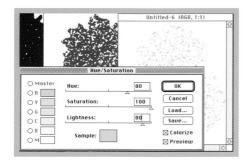

Step 16.

Return to the middle layer of leaves. They should still be selected, but if they aren't, use the Magic Wand tool and the Similar command from the Select menu to select all the mid-tone green leaves.

Step 17.

Choose **Copy** from the **Edit** menu (or press Command-C).

Step 18.

Activate the window with the thick, dark base of leaves.

Step 19.

Choose **Paste** from the **Edit** menu and position the mid-tone green leaves inside of the dark leafy background leaves. Your tree is starting to look more three-dimensional already.

Tip: You may want to choose **Hide Edges** from the **Select** menu to get a clearer picture of the selection as you change it in these steps.

Step 20.

Next, activate the lightest leaves the same way, using the Magic Wand tool and the Similar command from the Select menu.

Tip: If the Magic Wand tool selects all the leaves and the background with them, double-click the Magic Wand tool to change the settings. Make the Tolerance 1 and disable Anti-aliasing. Then try selecting the leaves again. Sometimes you have to play with the tolerance setting to adjust how much of a tonal range the Magic Wand will select.

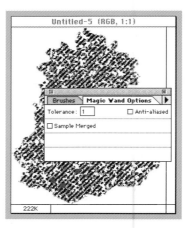

Step 21.

Choose **Copy** from the **Edit** menu.

Step 22.

Activate the original base image and choose **Paste** from the **Edit** menu to paste the highlight leaves over the existing image.

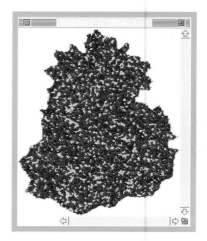

This looks OK, but could use that one final touch to really finish it off.

Step 23.

While the highlight leaves are still selected, select the Gradient tool.

Step 24.

In the Brushes palette, set the Opacity to 30% and the mode to Luminosity.

Step 25.

Drag from the bottom up across the image to mute the lower leaves in the image.

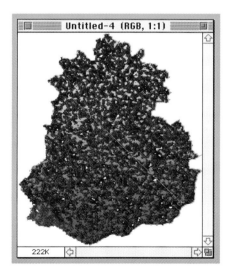

Step 26.

Repeat this a couple of times until you achieve the results that look best to you.

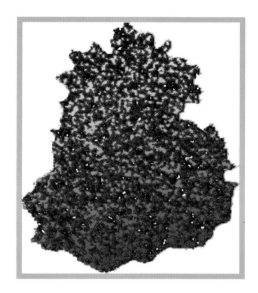

So far, you have a perfectly acceptable method of illustrating bushes and foliage textures. But what about the basic tree trunks? Let's add that now.

Step 27.

If you're satisfied with the way the foliage has turned out, copy it to the original 640-by-480-pixel image. Do this by using the Magic Wand tool to select just the background of the bush image.

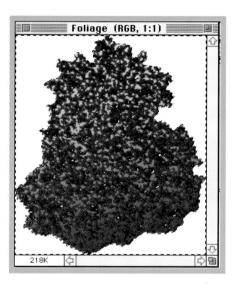

Step 28.

Choose **Similar** from the **Select** menu to include all the white specks in the interior of the biomass.

Step 29.

Choose **Inverse** from the **Select** menu.

Step 30.

Choose **Copy** from the **Edit** menu. Activate the original starting image and paste it into place there. Give yourself enough vertical space underneath to place a respectable tree trunk.

Step 31.

As you did when you created a two-dimensional silhouette version of the tree, use the Lasso tool to select a trunk-shaped area that extends up into the leafy area.

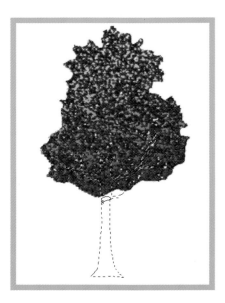

Step 32.

Choose **Fill** from the **Edit** menu to fill the selected shape with the foreground color.

Tip: You could stop here, but why not fill the tree trunk selection with a small amount of random noise, and then apply a motion blur filter by using the Blur and Motion Blur options from the Filter menu? Then you can color the image by using the Adjust and Hue/Saturation options from the Image menu (be sure to click the Preview and Colorize check boxes). Texturize even further by using the Sharpen and Sharpen More options from the Filter menu.

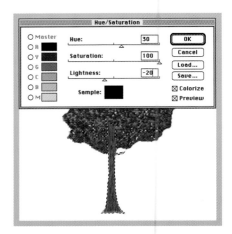

Step 33.

To finish off the illustration, use the Lasso tool again to select and copy some smaller leafy areas to clone and paste over the overly-exposed tree trunk.

Step 34.

Use the Magic Wand tool to select the entire background.

Step 35.

Choose **Inverse** from the **Select** menu to reselect the tree.

Step 36.

Copy and paste the tree into a new document, and then save it in the Library folder.

My Work ▼		⊂□ X-30
		Eject
		Desktop
		New 📁
Save this document as:		Cancel
Leafy Green Tree		Save
Format: TIFF ▼		

Now that you know how, it's easy to make your own little forest whenever you need to add some greenery to an illustration.

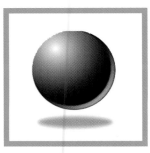

Chapter 6

Creating 3-D Objects with Photoshop

In this chapter, we'll create some common objects that you can use over and over in your work. We'll start with some simple cubes and progress through cones spheres and, finally, create some full, planetary scenes. All of these objects are really quite simple once you learn how to make them. And, after you get the objects created, you can apply all the ready-made custom textures we've made to them, creating entirely new looks.

Creating a Cube

Cubes are regularly shaped, which makes them predictable and easy to visualize. Solid-looking cubes are also remarkably easy to create, using a few simple steps. You can easily apply your own custom-made textures to them. Photoshop affords you a lot of freedom in perspective when you are creating cubes.

To create a cube, follow these steps:

Step 1.

Create a new document in Photoshop measuring six inches square in RGB Color mode with a resolution of 72 pixels/inch.

Step 2.

Hold down the Shift key and use the Rectangular Marquee tool to create a perfect square in the center of your work area. Leave plenty of space around the square because you will need it for some of the manipulations in this exercise.

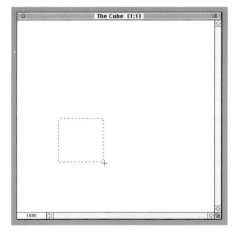

Next, add a graduated color to the area. Set the foreground/background color swatches to black and white. In this exercise, you work in black and white grayscales and add color later, but you can always do the same tricks in color.

Step 3.

Using the Gradient tool, drag diagonally across the selection to graduate the color. Try dragging the tool past the edge of the selection, beyond the borders.

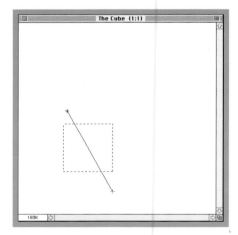

The Gradient tool creates a complete gradation starting where you first click and ending when you release the mouse button. If you click and drag to a place outside of the selection, the selection displays only the parts of the graduation inside the selection's borders.

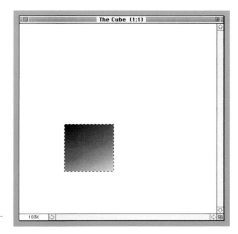

Step 4.

Choose **Copy** from the **Edit** menu. You'll use this square shape again in a moment.

Step 5.

While the square is still selected, choose **Skew** from the **Effects** sub-menu of the **Image** menu.

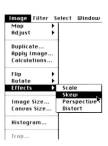

Little square handles appear at all four corners of the square.

Step 6.

Drag one of the handles down to create a skewed polygon.

Step 7.

Click the center of the altered image to implement the change.

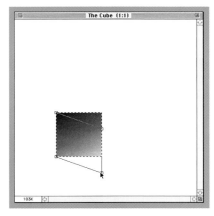

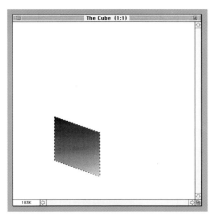

Step 8.

While the polygon is still selected, hold down the Option key and click on the object. This makes a clone of the object.

Step 9.

Hold down the Shift key and drag the selection to the right until the two objects share a common edge.

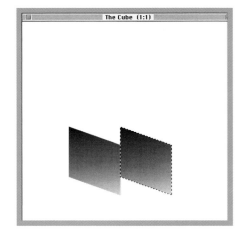

Step 10.

Choose **Horizontal** from the **Flip** sub-menu of the **Image** menu. The selection is flipped horizontally on its center axis, and shares a common edge with the other selection.

Step 11.

Next, you need to make the new section look less artificial. Use the Gradient tool to drag a new gradation into the selection. Drag diagonally in a downwards direction, as shown below.

This subtle change in gradation between the two sections makes them appear a little more natural and gives the joint between them a harder edge.

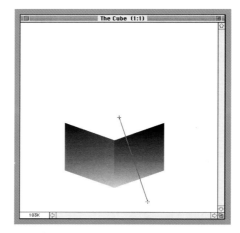

Next, you need to add the top of the cube. This is pretty easy, and there's a little trick you can do to add more realism and dimension to the image.

Step 12.

Choose **Paste** from the **Edit** menu. This produces a copy of the original cube saved to the Clipboard.

Step 13.

Choose **Arbitrary** from the **Rotate** submenu of the **Image** menu. Define the degree of rotation as 45° CW.

You want to rotate this square selection 45° clockwise so that its bottom corner matches with the corner where the two existing sides already meet.

Step 14.

Move the rotated square down into position where the two square sides meet.

Step 15.

Choose **Scale** from the **Effects** submenu of the **Image** menu.

Step 16.

You want to resize the rotated square so that it perfectly forms the top panel of the cube.

Use the handles to drag the left and right sides of the scale selection to align with the edges of the cube. Then, drag the top handles down until the bottom edges of the rotated square abut the top edges of the cube sides.

Voilà! The illusion of depth is complete.

Tip: When you resize the top panel of the cube, manipulate the corners of the panels so that the outside corners are right on the outside top corners of the sides. Then bring up the bottom just a bit so that there is one pixel between the center corner of the top panel and the joint of the two sides. The selection will anti-alias, that is, pixels in various shades of gray are automatically placed to create a smooth edge. This gives the joint between the sides and top a very subtle enhancement.

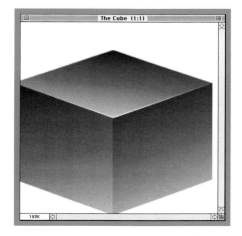

Saving the Cube Paths

Someday, you may want to reuse this cube, changing its color or texture.

To do that, it would be handy to be able to reselect the sides of the cube. Selecting each individual side of the cube, you can place different textures on each side. You can do this by using the Paths palette and saving paths for the illustration. Follow these steps:

Step 1.

Choose **Show Paths** from the **Window** menu.

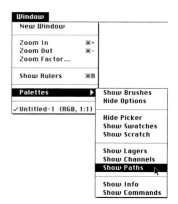

Step 2.

Using the Pen tool, click on all four corners of one side of the cube to create a path.

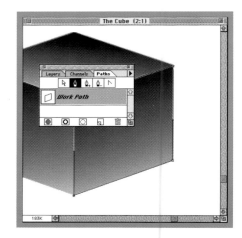

Because you're just clicking once at each point (without moving the Pen tool before releasing the mouse button) the Pen tool is connecting each point with a straight path (or line) that can be saved.

Step 3.

Click the arrow in the top right of the Paths palette. A pop-up menu appears.

Step 4.

Choose Save Path and name the path anything you like.

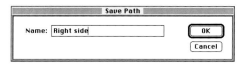

Step 5.

Repeat steps 1 to 4 for each face of the cube. For this exercise, you should end up with three paths.

You might also want to copy or move the entire object. You can do this by creating a path that outlines the entire object.

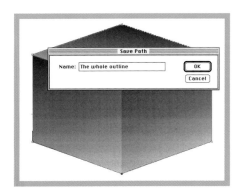

You can add color or a new shade to any panel by choosing its path in the Paths palette and changing it into a selection. Follow these steps:

Step 1.

Click the path you want to change.

Step 2.

Choose the arrow tool in the Paths palette. A pop-up menu appears. Choose Make Selection.

Step 3.

At this point, you can add color, shading, textures, or whatever effects you want.

Step 4.

Complete the image by coloring the remaining panels and adding a fuzzy drop shadow.

Adding Texture to the Cube

You add texture to the cube the same way you would add color or a gradient fill. Create a perfect square selection and fill it with one of the patterns or textures that you have already made. You do this by opening the texture or pattern and selecting the image using the Rectangular Marquee tool. In this exercise, use the Brick pattern you created in Chapter 4.

Step 1.

Once you've selected your pattern image, choose **Define Pattern** from the **Edit** menu.

Step 2.

Create a new document in Photoshop. Hold down the Shift key and use the Rectangular Marquee tool to create a perfect square in the middle of your work area. Choose **Fill** from the **Edit** menu to fill the square selection with the pattern.

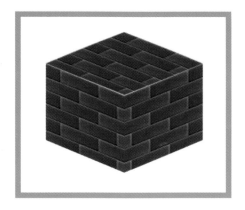

Step 3.

Complete the steps in the previous section "Creating a Cube" to create a textured cube.

Not bad, but it could use a little more depth. You can enhance the dimension by simulating the effects of lighting with gradient fills. Follow these steps:

Step 1.

Create paths outlining each of the three panels (as explained in the previous section) Next, you'll turn them into selections and add a graduated shade to each side.

Step 2.

Choose **Show Brushes** from the **View** menu to display the Brushes palette.

This palette enables you to define opacity for the fill as well as a style of application. You can, for example, you can apply the graduated fill only where it will darken the values of pixels in the selection. You can also choose to lighten only, or you can adjust the hue and brightness.

Step 3.

To apply the illusion of brightness, choose Lighten from the pop-up menu in the Brushes palette. Set the Opacity to 30%, and then apply the graduated tone.

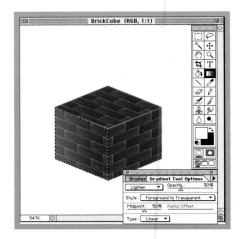

Step 4.

To apply the illusion of shadow on the shadow side, choose Darken from the Brushes palette and repeat the effect on the right side.

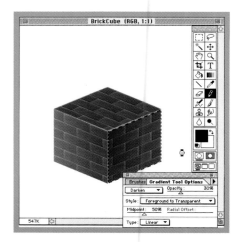

You can finish the image by adding one of the other dimension-enhancing tricks, such as a shadow.

Creating a Cone

In this section, you learn how to make realistic-looking cones using paint tools and filters. Follow these steps:

Step 1.

Create a new document measuring 6 by 6 inches, with a resolution of 72 pixels/inch. Make sure that the mode is RGB Color if you're working in color, or grayscale if you're working in black and white.

Step 2.

Use the Rectangular Marquee tool to select about a vertical third of the work area.

Step 3.

Make sure that the foreground/background color selection swatches are set to black and white (click the Default Colors icon in the tool palette if necessary), and then use the Gradient tool to create a gradation from left to right across the selection area.

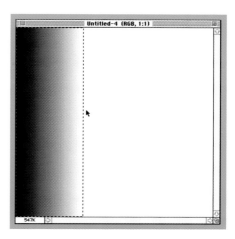

Step 4.

Use the Rectangular Marquee tool to select two-thirds of the remaining area.

Step 5.

Reverse the foreground/background colors by clicking the Switch Colors icon in the tool palette. Fill this area with an identical graduated fill.

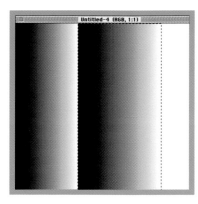

Step 6.

Reverse the foreground and background colors again. Select the remaining white space and fill it with a gradation.

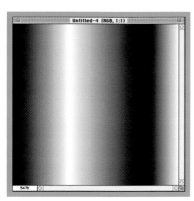

Step 7.

Choose **Select All** from the **Edit** menu (or use the keyboard shortcut Command-A) to select the entire image.

Step 8.

Choose **Perspective** from the **Effects** submenu of the **Image** menu.

Step 9.

Click the square selection handle in the top right corner of the selection and drag it to the left. Notice how the opposite corner moves inward at the same rate, making the selection symmetrical. When the points meet in the center, release the mouse button.

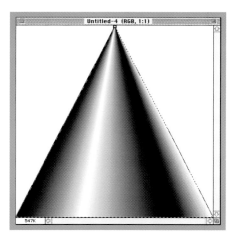

Step 10.

If you want to make the cone narrower, you can also drag the lower corners.

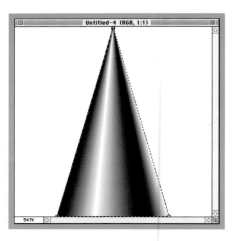

Step 11.

Click once in the center of the selection to lock it into place.

Now you have a shiny metallic-looking texture in a cone.

Enhancing the Effect

This is a nice effect, but let's add a little realism by making it appear truly three dimensional. Follow these steps:

Step 1.

While the texture is still selected, choose **Copy** from the **Edit** menu (or press Command-C). This places a copy of the selection onto the clipboard.

Next, you'll form the bottom edge of the cone using the Elliptical Marquee tool and the Lasso tool.

Step 2.

Use the Elliptical Marquee tool to create a wide, shallow ellipse as shown below.

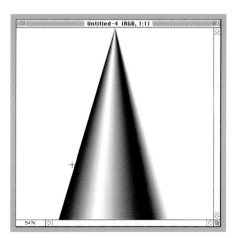

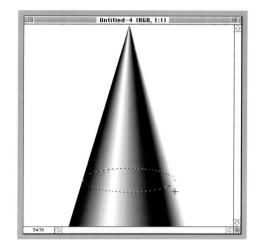

This may take a few tries to get it just right, so don't be shy about choosing Undo from the Edit menu.

Step 3.

Here's where it gets a little tricky. Select the Lasso tool, hold down the Shift key (to tell Photoshop that you want to add to the current selection), and then drag the cursor within the ellipse to a point near the right edge of the ellipse.

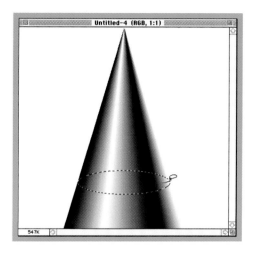

Step 4.

When you get to the very edge of the ellipse, press and hold down the Option key, and then let go of the mouse button.

Step 5.

Move the Lasso tool to the tip of the cone.

You will see that the selection is still active. A line connects the end point of the selection, where you first pressed the Option key, to the cursor location.

Step 6.

Continue holding down the Option key, and click the tip of the cone (be sure to let go of the mouse button). This anchors the selection there.

Step 7.

Move the cursor to the opposite edge of the original elliptical selection.

Step 8.

Now press and hold down the mouse button while you drag the cursor into the ellipse.

Step 9.

Let go of the mouse button, and then let go of the Option and the Shift keys to complete the selection.

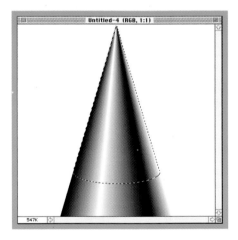

Tip: At this point, you might want to choose Show Paths from the Window menu and save this selection as a path for later use.

Step 10.

To finish off the shape, choose **Inverse** from the **Selection** menu. The whole background area (minus the cone shape) is selected.

Step 11.

Make sure your background color is white, then press the Delete key to remove the selection. You're left with a perfect, symmetrical cone shape.

Step 12.

Choose **Inverse** from the **Select** menu to reselect the cone shape. You can move it around in the work area just to make sure that it's real.

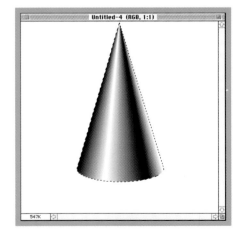

Step 13.

Choose **Copy** from the **Edit** menu. This will save a backup copy to the clipboard to use if you need it.

Step 14.

Choose **Save** from the **File** menu to save a copy of the image for you to use.

Adding Lighting Effects

You can apply some simple lighting effects to enhance the realism of the cone. Let's start with the simplest of effects, the fuzzy drop shadow. Follow these steps:

Step 1.

Use the Elliptical Marquee tool to create a wide, shallow ellipse right under the base of the cone.

Step 2.

Choose **Feather** from the **Select** menu and set the feather value to 3 pixels.

Step 3.

Make sure that the foreground color is set to black. Choose **Fill** from the **Edit** menu. Set the Opacity to 75% (or whatever you think might look good).

You can also create a cast shadow. Revert the image back to the cone or delete everything on the page and paste in the original cone image that should still be on the Clipboard. Follow these steps to create a cast shadow for your cone:

Step 1.

Using the Lasso tool, hold down the Option key while you click one side of the cone base, click again at a point behind the cone, and click again at the opposite side of the cone base to complete a triangular shape that overlaps the base of the cone.

Step 2.

Make sure that the foreground color is still set to black. Choose **Fill** from the **Edit** menu. Set the Opacity to 75% and fill the area.

Step 3.

Deselect the area by clicking anywhere outside of it or by choosing **None** from the **Select** menu.

Step 4.

Now that you have the shadow painted in, choose **Paste** from the **Edit** menu to replace the original cone image back over the image on the screen.

Step 5.

Choose **Hide Edges** from the **Select** menu (or press Command-H) to hide the "marching ants" around the selection.

Step 6.

If your pasted cone doesn't exactly match the position of your original, you can use the arrow keys to nudge the selection into place on the image.

Creating a Sphere

As you have learned, it's easy to create your own simple objects in Adobe Photoshop. Unlike a 3-D modeling program—a program that allows you to create three-dimensional objects and then apply a variety of textures and lighting to them—Photoshop serves as a sophisticated painting program. Creating simple geometric shapes in Photoshop is a breeze if you know the right steps.

Creating a simple sphere is easy. It's basically a perfect circle that has some special lighting and shading applied to it to simulate the illusion of three dimensions. In this exercise, you start with a simple sphere and progressively add simple effects to enhance its realism. Follow these steps:

Step 1.

Create a new document. Make it perfectly square by entering equal dimensions for the width and height in the New dialog box.

Step 2.

Using the Elliptical Marquee tool, hold down the Shift key and create a perfect circle. Be sure to leave some room around the outside. You will use this area later on to add a few enhancements.

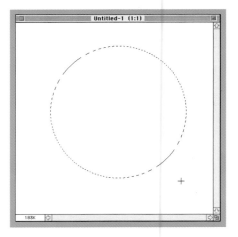

Step 3.

In the tool palette, set the foreground and background colors to black and white. (A shortcut is to click the Default Colors icon in the lower left corner of the tool palette).

Step 4.

Click the Switch Colors icon to change the foreground to white and the background to black.

Step 5.

Double-click the Gradient tool, and click the Radial radio button.

Step 6.

Click OK.

Step 7.

In your Brushes palette, set your Opacity to 100% and your mode to Normal. Position the cursor within the circular selection area and drag to apply the gradation.

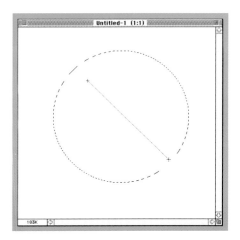

The origin point (the place where you click first before beginning the drag) will be white, and the end point (where you release the mouse button) will be solid black with any further contiguous areas filling in solid black.

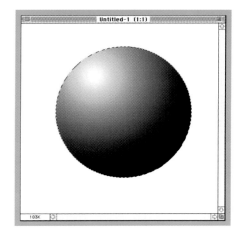

You can try adjusting the percentage values in the Midpoint Skew and Radial Offset fields and reapplying the graduation for different effects.

Adding Reflections

That was simple enough. You can make the sphere look a bit more lifelike by adding a reflection to the outer edge of the sphere. This task is a little tougher, requiring some channel work, so hold onto your tall pointed wizard's hat and follow these steps:

Step 1.

If the sphere is still selected, great. If not, choose the Magic Wand tool and click in the background of the image. Make sure that the tolerance for the Magic Wand tool is set to 1 by double-clicking the tool before using it.

Step 2.

Choose **Inverse** from the **Selection** menu to invert the selected area from the background to the sphere. This method is easier than trying to select the sphere using the Elliptical Marquee tool.

Next, you need to scale the selection area without moving the image in it. To do this, you have to create a new channel.

Step 3.

Choose **Show Channels** from the **Window** menu.

Step 4.

Click the arrow in the corner of the **Show Channels** menu.

Step 5.

Choose New Channel from the pop-up menu that appears.

Step 6.

Name this channel anything you want.

Step 7.

Select the new channel by clicking its name in the palette. You will see the selection outline, but not the image in it. (The image is still in the RGB channel; you're in the new channel you just created.)

Step 8.

Choose **Scale** from the **Effects** submenu of the **Image** menu.

Step 9.

Hold down the Shift key and drag the lower right corner handle up and to the left a bit to rescale the image. Click inside the selection to cause the effect to take place.

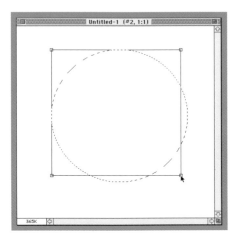

Step 10.

Return to the RGB channel by clicking its name in the Channels palette (or pressing Command-0).

You can see how the selection has changed, but not the image.

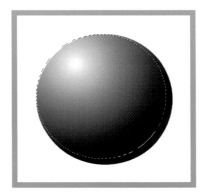

Step 11.

Using the Magic Wand tool, hold down the Shift key while you click in the white background area.

Using the Shift key this way enables you to add to any selection, and the Magic Wand tool selects all the contiguous white pixels in the background. Now, the selected area consists of the sphere and the background (without the crescent area around the lower right half of the sphere).

The next step should be pretty self-evident. Because you're going to add some shading to the crescent area (which is currently not selected) you need to invert the selection.

Step 12.

Choose **Inverse** from the **Select** menu. Aha! Only the crescent area is selected.

Next, just to add one more hint of realism to this, you'll go back to the extra channel and scale down the crescent selection a bit.

Step 13.

Return to the new channel. Choose **Scale** from the **Effects** submenu of the **Image** menu.

Step 14.

Hold down the Shift key and drag the handle a bit to rescale the image. Make this a small, subtle change. You're trying to leave an edge of pixels still visible behind the selection. Click inside the selection to cause the effect to take place.

Step 15.

Return to the RGB channel.

And now for the finishing touches.

Step 16.

Double-click the Gradient tool. Click the Linear radio button.

```
┌──────── Gradient Tool Options ────────┐
│                                        │
│  ┌─Style──────────────────┐  ┌──────┐ │
│  │ ⦿ Normal               │  │  OK  │ │
│  │ ○ Clockwise Spectrum   │  └──────┘ │
│  │ ○ Counterclockwise Spectrum│ ┌────────┐│
│  │                        │  │ Cancel │ │
│  └────────────────────────┘  └────────┘ │
│  ┌─Type────────────────────┐            │
│  │ ⦿ Linear                │            │
│  │ ○ Radial                │            │
│  └─────────────────────────┘            │
│                                          │
│  Midpoint Skew: [ 50 ] %                │
│  Radial Offset: [    ] %                │
└──────────────────────────────────────────┘
```

Step 17.

Choose **Feather** from the **Select** menu. Set the feather value to 2 pixels.

Step 18.

Click OK.

Step 19.

Drag diagonally upwards and to the left to create a gradient fill inside the selected area. Experiment with the gradient fill by dragging from different origin points and making longer and shorter drags to create smoother or more abrupt gradations.

Adding a Drop Shadow

Sometimes the best way to add life to an image is not by affecting the image itself, but by manipulating areas outside of the image. This section presents is the easiest, cheapest, quickest way to add more life to the image of the sphere: adding a drop shadow. Follow these steps:

Step 1.

Use the Elliptical Marquee tool to create an ellipse beneath the sphere.

Step 2.

Make sure that the foreground color selection is black.

Step 3.
Step 3.

Choose **Fill** from the **Edit** menu. Change the Opacity to 50% to fill the selection with a 50% shade of black.

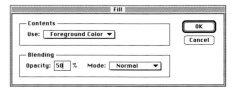

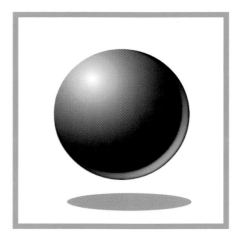

This is a nice effect, but you can make it even more lifelike by feathering the shadow.

Step 4.

Choose **Feather** from the **Select** menu. Set the value to 6 pixels.

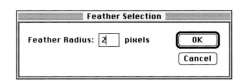

Step 5.

Choose **Fill** from the **Edit** menu and click OK.

Save this image so that you can use it later.

Creating a Moon

In this section, you'll learn a fun technique that you can use to create planetary ornaments for any outer space or science fiction illustration. With this technique, you can create airless moons, planetoids, asteroids, and comets, as well as planetary bodies with atmospheres and geological character. Here's how to do it:

Step 1.

Create a new document measuring 400 by 400 pixels in RGB Color mode, with a resolution of 72 pixels/inch.

Step 2.

Use the Elliptical Marquee tool to select an area inside this image. Hold down the Shift key to maintain equal proportions, constraining it to a perfect circle.

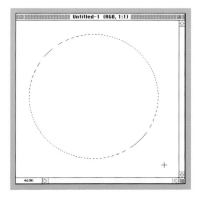

remarkable formations. Later, you add some variations to this effect.

Step 4.

Choose **Emboss** from the **Stylize** submenu of the **Filter** menu. Set the angle to 135°, the height to 1 pixel, and the amount to 100%.

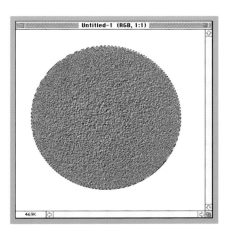

Step 3.

Add some noise to the selection. Choose **Add Noise** from the **Noise** submenu of the **Filter** menu. Set the amount to 999 and the distribution to Gaussian for an even, but dense, sprinkling of noise.

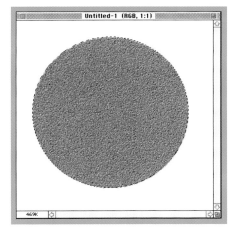

Step 6.

Reapply the same filter by pressing Command-F.

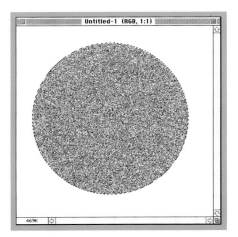

A pretty nice effect—if your career plans involve illustrating the flat sides of rotary sander discs. If you want to create a planet, though, you need to add some dimension.

Step 5.

Choose **Spherize** from the **Distort** submenu of the **Filter** menu. Set the amount to 100% and click the Normal radio button.

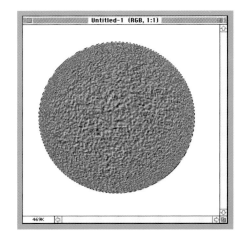

Next, you make the first step toward geological design. First, you make the planet fairly smooth in its geology, without any

This has the effect of really stretching the interior pixels while compressing the pixels around the outer edges.

Unless they are artificially colored, most deep-space images sent back by NASA/JPL probes are flat grayscale. So, let's remove some of the color from this image (you can always recolor it later).

Step 7.

Choose **Hue/Saturation** from the **Adjust** submenu of the **Image** menu. Make sure that only the Preview checkbox is clicked. Set the Saturation field to -100.

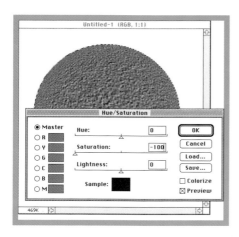

So far, so good. Next, you'll add some nice gradient lighting to the object, creating the illusion of a three-dimensional sphere.

Step 8.

Double-click the Gradient tool and change the mode from Linear to Radial.

Step 9.

Set the foreground and background colors so that white is in the foreground and black is in the background. (As a shortcut, you can click the Default Colors icon in the lower left area of the swatches section, then click the Switch Colors icon in the upper right area.)

Step 10.

Choose **Show Brushes** from the **Window** menu. The Brushes palette is displayed. Set the Opacity to 50% and the mode to Multiply.

Step 11.

Using the Gradient tool, drag from a spot in the upper left quarter of the moon to the bottom right edge. Note the foreground/background color selections and the brush settings in the Brush palette.

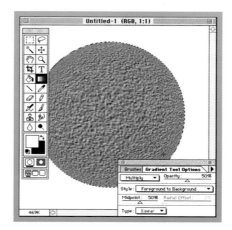

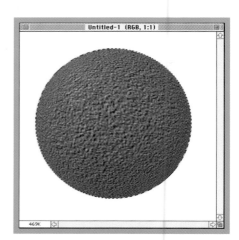

A nice and subtle effect. You can repeat this step until you have a sufficient contrast between the lighter and darker sides of the rocky sphere.

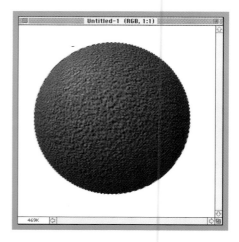

Step 12.

Choose **Inverse** from the **Select** menu and then press the Delete key. If the foreground and background colors are still white and black, this replaces the white background with a completely dark one.

Step 13.

Use the Magic Wand tool to click anywhere in the black background. Select **Inverse** from the **Select** menu to reselect the moon. Choose **Scale** from the **Effects** submenu of the **Image** menu Reduce the size of the moon in relationship to the image area.

At this point, the moon is still selected, so if you want to color it, blur the details, or add another radial gradient fill, this is the perfect time.

You should select just the moon itself, without the background, and save it in your library of objects. This moon looks great pasted into any scenery.

You can enhance the look of your homemade moon by changing some of the filter settings as you create it. Following are a few quick enhancements.

Adding an Atmosphere

You can add a ghostly veil of an atmosphere to your moon. Follow these steps:

Step 1.

In the Brushes palette, set the mode to Normal and leave the Opacity at 50% (or less, for a more subtle effect).

Step 2.

Apply a radial gradient fill to the moon as you did previously.

Making the Terrain Rockier

How about rockier terrain? This technique is a spherized variant of the stucco texture you learned about in Chapter 3. You achieve the levels of coarseness by controlling the amount of diffusion and emboss depth. Follow these steps:

For this exercise you will almost have to start from scratch, but if your planet is still selected from the previous exercise, you can choose Save As from the File menu to creating a new copy of the document with a different name, and continue working on the original.

Step 1.

Recreate the basic technique by following Steps 1 through 3 in the "Creating a Moon" section described earlier.

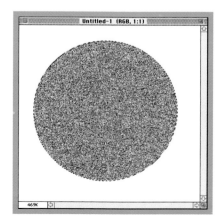

Step 2.

Choose **Gaussian Blur** from the **Blur** submenu of the **Filter** menu. Set the radius to 4 to spread the pixels.

Step 3.

To add some harsh texture to the blended disk, choose **Diffuse** from the **Stylize** submenu of the **Filter** menu. Click the Normal radio button.

Step 4.

Using the Command-F keyboard shortcut, reapply this filter six or seven times.

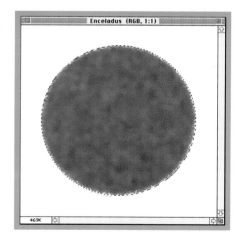

Step 5.

Choose **Brightness/Contrast** from the **Adjust** submenu of the **Image** menu (or press Command-B). Set the Contrast value to 100.

Step 6.

Choose **Emboss** from the **Stylize** submenu of the **Filter** menu to create a nice, rough, 3-D texture.

Step 7.

Choose **Spherize** from the **Distort** submenu of the **Filter** menu. Set the amount to 100%.

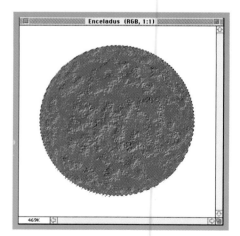

Further Enhancing the Image

You can make your image a little more real by removing most of the color range. Follow these steps:

Step 1.

Choose **Hue/Saturation** from the **Adjust** submenu of the **Image** menu (or press Command-U). Make sure that the Colorize checkbox is not clicked. Remove all the saturation from the image by setting the Saturation slider to -100.

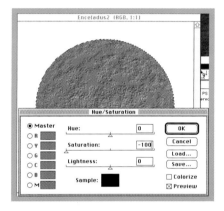

Step 2.

Double-click the Gradient tool and set its mode to Radial.

Step 3.

Select **Show Brushes** from the **Window** menu. The Brushes palette is displayed.

Step 4.

On the Brushes palette, set the Opacity to 50% and the mode to Multiply.

Step 5.

Use the Gradient tool to drag across the sphere to create a subtle radial gradation.

Tip: You can make the effect more subtle by setting the Opacity to a lower value and reapplying the gradation a few times. This gives you a more precise control over the density of the gradation you apply.

Changing the Highlights

You may want to enhance the contrast of the highlights in the image, depending on the mood of the illustration. You could use the Brightness/Contrast controls from the Image menu, but there is a more subtle option. Follow these steps:

Step 1.

Choose **Curves** from the **Adjust** submenu of the **Image** menu.

Step 2.

Set and adjust an alternate contrast curve. This gives you more subtle control over the entire grayscale range in the selection.

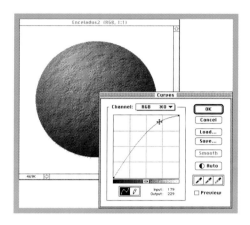

Step 3.

As before, you may want to resize the moon against a black background and save it into your personal library of objects.

Chapter 7

Creating Special Effects

In one sense, this entire work is about special effects in Adobe Photoshop. Everything you have accomplished so far is the result of applying special effects through filters and manipulation in this program. Some of these effects are the outcome of several steps of complementary effects layered on top of each other to produce even more complex and spectacular effects. The intention has been to create a foundation of skills on which you can build your own individual bag of tricks and create your own illustrations.

This chapter shows you how to create some amazing visual effects that you can use to enhance any digital illustration. You learn how to create glowing and translucent effects, which can add depth to two-dimensional objects. You also learn how to create some surreal effects, such as turning any object or texture to liquid with ripples and reflections.

Most of the effects are simple applications of common filters, but they are sure to surprise you in their ultimate results. Building the texture is often secondary to what you're planning to do with it. You can achieve some dynamite effects by layering some illustrative techniques onto some fairly simple textural effects.

Creating Glows

A glow is a simple effect that can add magic and mystery to special illustrations. In this section, you learn to add a soft glow to any part of your illustrations, regardless of the background.

This example uses objects and effects you have already created and saved in other chapters. If you skipped any of these chapters, now would be a good time to go back and create some of the effects used here. You can always use an extra effect or object in your personal library.

For the first exercise, open the sphere you created in Chapter 6, and then follow these steps:

Step 1.

Select just the sphere by using a constrained Elliptical Marquee tool. Or, you can use the Magic Wand tool to select just the background and then choose **Inverse** from the **Select** menu.

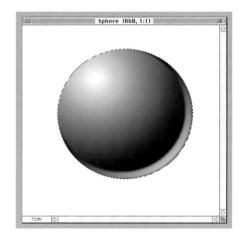

Step 2.

Choose **Copy** from the **Edit** menu (or press Command-C) to copy the sphere to the clipboard.

Step 3.

Choose **Close** from the **File** menu.

Step 4.

Now create a new document measuring 640 by 480 pixels in RGB Color mode, with a resolution of 72 pixels/inch.

Because a glow is kind of a spacey effect, for this exercise let's create a mildly spacey background.

Step 5.

Choose **Add Noise** from the **Noise** submenu of the **Filter** menu. Set the Noise value to 999 and choose Gaussian distribution to fill the background with random noise.

Step 6.

Choose **Diffuse** from the **Stylize** submenu of the **Filter** menu. Click the Darken only radio button.

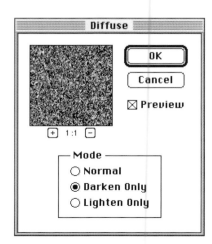

Step 7.

Repeat this filter by pressing the keyboard shortcut Command-F a few times until you get a reasonable-looking starry background.

Step 8.

Choose **Blur** from the **Blur** submenu of the **Filter** menu to apply a mellow blur.

Step 9.

Press Command-F a few times to soften the effect a bit.

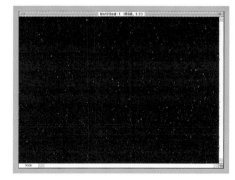

Step 10.

Choose **Paste** from the **Edit** menu to paste a copy of the chrome sphere into your new document.

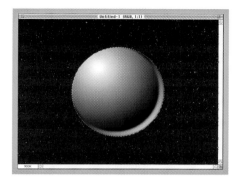

Now for the glow part. Follow these steps:

Step 1.

Choose **Feather** from the **Select** menu and apply a wide feather radius to the selection. For this example, try a radius of 24 pixels.

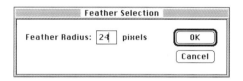

There are basically two methods to add a glow to your sphere. You can either remove the feathered selection, exposing the background color, making that the glow. But that's a quick and dirty method that does not offer much control over the amount and translucency of the glow.

Instead, let's place a well-controlled and expert glow around the sphere.

Step 2.

Decide what color you want the sphere to glow. Click the foreground color swatch in the tool palette and choose a brightly contrasting foreground color.

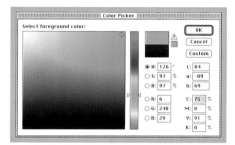

Step 3.

Choose **Fill** from the **Edit** menu to fill the feathered selection with the foreground color. Experiment with the Opacity setting to adjust how intense you want the glow to be. You can also adjust the Feather radius to extend the width of the glow.

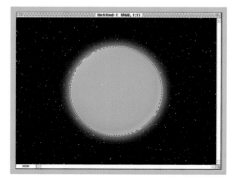

Step 4.

Choose **Paste** from the **Edit** menu to paste the original sphere over the glowing selection to complete the effect.

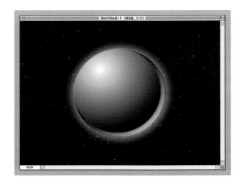

Note: If you want the glow surrounding the selection to carry into the sphere you paste into the image, use the Paste Into command instead of the Paste command. This allows a more subtle transformation between foreground and background.

Adding a Glow to Type

You can create some very dramatic effects by applying this same technique to type. Follow these steps to create the background:

Step 1.

Choose **Add Noise** from the **Noise** submenu of the **Filter** menu. Set the Noise value to 999 and select Gaussian distribution to fill the background with random noise.

Step 2.

Choose **Diffuse** from the **Stylize** submenu of the **Filter** menu. Click the Darken Only radio button.

Step 3.

Repeat this filter by pressing the keyboard shortcut Command-F a few times until you get a reasonable looking starry background.

Step 4.

Choose **Blur** from the **Blur** submenu of the **Filter** menu to apply a mellow blur.

Step 5.

Press Command-F a few times to soften the effect a bit.

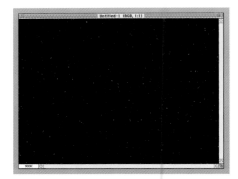

In this background, you will create some type objects and perform several manipulations with them. To make a simple and reselectable type object, you will create it in a new channel. Follow these steps:

Step 1.

Choose **Show Channels** from the **Window** menu.

Step 2.

Create a new channel using the pop-up menu in the Channel palette.

Step 3.

Using the Type tool, create a bold type object in the new channel.

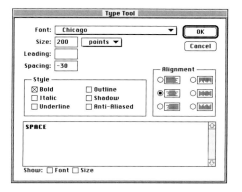

This example uses Chicago type. Although it isn't too pretty, it's native to all Macintosh computers.

Step 4.

Return to the RGB channel. Notice that the letter forms are still selected even though the type exists in the extra channel.

Step 5.

Choose **Copy** from the **Edit** menu to copy the text objects to the clipboard.

Step 6.

Choose **Feather** from the **Select** menu. Set the Feather Radius to 12 pixels for a medium-grade glow.

Step 7.

Choose a new foreground color just for variety's sake.

Step 8.

Choose **Fill** from the **Edit** menu to apply a smooth glow around the letter forms.

Your letter forms appear fuzzy and indistinct, but remember that you still have a clean reference copy in the correct position on the extra channel.

Tip: Using the Opacity setting in the Fill dialog box gives you a great deal of control over the effect. You can also intensify the effect by reapplying the fill a second time. In this instance you may want to try that.

Step 9.

Choose a new foreground color that contrasts with the glow color you just created.

Step 10.

Choose **Stroke** from the **Edit** menu. Set the width to 3 pixels and click the Center radio button. This applies a simple stroke around the selection.

You can create new effects by reselecting the letter forms in the extra channel. Use the Magic Wand tool to click once on a single letter, and then choose **Similar** from the **Select** menu. This works better than clicking in the background and choosing **Inverse** from the **Select** menu because it selects the letter forms alone without including the white spaces in the letters A and P.

Because you can reselect text as often as you like, you can apply and reapply a variety of effects to the selection to finish the illustration.

A simple enhancement is to add a gradient fill to the selection. Follow these steps:

Step 1.

Make sure that your foreground and background colors are set to white and black.

Step 2.

While the text is still selected, double-click the Gradient tool and click the Radial radio button to set the style to radial.

Step 3.

In the Brushes palette, set the Opacity to 30% and the mode to Lighten.

Step 4.

Drag the Gradient tool across the selection and voilà!

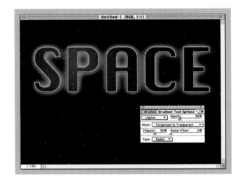

Creating Glings

Another great enhancement (which is often overdone by art students with their first new airbrush) is the gentle art of adding glings to the illustration.

Glings are the bright reflection flares you see on chrome objects in direct sunlight, not unlike chrome tailfin trim from a '63 Cadillac. Used in moderation, they look great almost anywhere.

The quick and easy (and imprecise) way to do this is to deselect everything and use the airbrush tool with a light foreground color and a broad brush shape to indiscriminately add glings on the corners of all the letters. Too easy, and a little cheap looking.

To add professional glings to your letter forms, follow these steps:

Step 1.

If the text shape is still selected, choose **Border** from the **Select** menu and create a 3-pixel selection around the edges of the type. (If the text isn't selected, use the methods discussed in the section on metals to reselect the text shape.)

Step 2.

Select a light foreground color. Choose **Show Brushes** from the **Window** menu.

Step 3.

Choose the Airbrush tool. When you switch to the Airbrush tool, you gain an adjustable Pressure slider in the Brushes palette. Make sure that the Pressure in the Brushes palette is set to a relatively low value (20-30%) so you can be subtle about how much color you're applying.

Step 4.

You may want to hide the edges of the selection marquee to get a clearer look at the selection you're painting (press Command-H).

Step 5.

Using the Airbrush tool, apply a little highlight to the border around the central focus area of the image, following the contours of the letter shape.

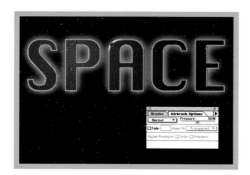

Not a bad touch of highlight for starters.

Step 6.

While the letter forms are still selected, choose **Feather** from the **Select** menu. Set the Feather radius to 4 pixels.

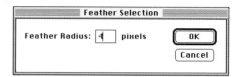

(Once again, you may want to hide the edges of the selection area for a better view of what you're doing.)

Step 7.

Reapply a little more highlight to the area you have already airbrushed, making a subtle glow around the selection. Be careful not to overpower the soft highlight you have already created. This is meant to be a very subtle accent to the effect.

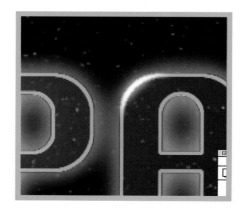

Step 8.

Choose a smaller brush shape and set the Pressure to 100%.

Step 9.

Deselect everything and blast one little airbrush spot at the center of the area you have been working on so far.

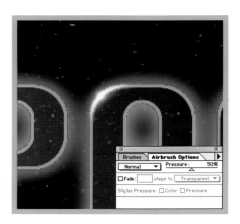

A perfect gling added to the text!

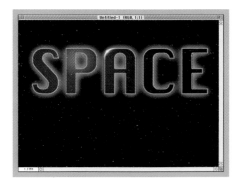

Adding Fuzzy Drop Shadows

Adding fuzzy drop shadow effects to any illustration is a technique that will set your work apart from everyone else's. And luckily for you, it's not that hard to master. It requires some careful attention to the steps, so follow along closely and enjoy the ride.

This simple technique involves a basic foundation technique that you can use with any Photoshop project. There are a couple of efficient ways to accomplish this effect. This exercise presents the easiest, most direct method first. Follow these steps:

Step 1.

Create a new document measuring 640 by 480 pixels, in RGB Color mode, with a resolution of 72 pixels/inch.

Step 2.

Select the Type tool and click somewhere roughly in the center of the work area.

The Type Tool dialog box appears. Enter font and size specifications for the type you are about to create.

Step 3.

Make sure that the Anti-aliased check box is not clicked. This will cause the type to look a little jagged initially, but it avoids an unpleasant white line around the edges of the letters when you paste them over another object later.

Step 4.

While the type is still selected, choose **Copy** from the **Edit** menu to copy the type object to the Clipboard. You'll need it to paste in later.

Step 5.

Next, you need to fill the selection with white so that the selection is the same color as the background. Choose white as the foreground color and, choose **Fill** from the **Edit** menu.

Step 6.

Now to add the fuzzy shadow. Choose **Feather** from the **Select** menu. Set the Feather value to 4.

Step 7.

Make sure that the foreground color is set to black. (You can click the Default Colors icon in the tool palette to set the foreground and background colors to black and white.)

Step 8.

Choose **Fill** from the **Edit** menu to fill the selection with a percentage of the black foreground color.

Step 9.

Choose **None** from the **Select** menu (or press Command-D) to deselect the shadow selection.

Step 10.

Choose **Paste** from the **Edit** menu. Your original copied selection appears on top of the shadow.

Step 11.

Move the cursor over the selection, changing the cursor to an arrow.

Step 12.

Click the selection and drag it into position above and to the left of the shadow.

Step 13.

While the selection is still active, you can adjust its position easily using the mouse, or by using the arrow keys on the keyboard to move the selection around one pixel at a time. Adjust the image to increase the illusion of depth and dimension.

Remember that, while the type object is selected, you can apply all manner of other tools and techniques (as you can with any other selection), such as gradient fills and strokes.

Creating Shapes from Textures

Now that you have the basics of fuzzy drop shadows figured out, let's apply the same technique to a textured background. Open a completed texture document that you have already created, or you can create a new one. For this exercise, use the sandstone texture that you created back in Chapter 3, "Creating Rocks and Gravel."

Follow these steps:

Step 1.

Choose the Lasso tool. Hold down the Option key as you click three points to create a triangular selection.

Step 2.

Choose **Copy** from the **Edit** menu to save a copy of this selection in the clipboard.

Step 3.

Choose **Feather** from the **Select** menu. Set the Feather radius to 6.

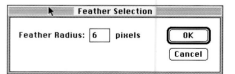

Step 4.

Choose **Fill** from the **Edit** menu and fill the selection with 50% black.

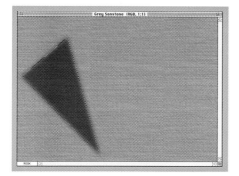

Step 5.

Choose **Paste** from the **Edit** menu to paste the triangular sandstone selection back into the image.

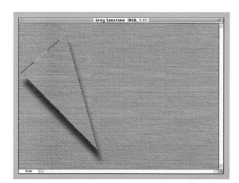

You may want to create some differentiation between the background sandstone and the pasted selection. You can apply a simple stroke around the selection, or you can apply a simple graduated tint using the Gradient tool.

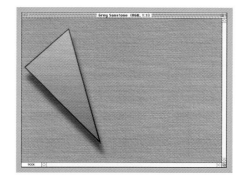

Don't be afraid to experiment and get the effect you want.

Creating a Cast Shadow

Creating a cast shadow is almost as easy as creating a drop shadow, and with a few extra steps, you can add a dimension of life that will set your art apart from everyone else's.

In this exercise, you'll learn how to create the basic shadow, and then you learn how to give it more life by using some simple but subtle enhancements.

Follow these steps:

Step 1.

Create a new document measuring 640 by 480 pixels in RGB Color mode, with a resolution of 72 pixels/inch.

Step 2.

Using the Type tool, create some type in the new document by clicking once in the center of the image area. For this demonstration, use one of the standard Macintosh fonts.

Step 3.

Choose **Copy** from the **Edit** menu to copy the text to the clipboard for later use.

Step 4.

While the type is still selected, either select a medium gray foreground color and then choose **Fill** from the **Edit** menu. Or choose **Brightness/Contrast** from the **Adjust** submenu of from the **Image** menu, and set the Brightness to 100%. Either method lets you create a medium gray selection that will become the cast shadow.

Step 5.

Choose **Skew** from the **Effects** submenu of the **Image** menu.

Step 6.

Drag one of the upper handles to the right to create a skewed selection. Click inside the selection to cause the change to take place.

Step 7.

Choose **None** from the **Select** menu to deselect the skewed type.

Step 8.

Choose **Paste** from the **Edit** menu to place the original type selection on top of the skewed light gray shadow.

Step 9.

Now, just for effect, choose a new foreground color.

Step 10.

Choose **Fill** from the **Edit** menu to change the color of the newly pasted-in type.

If you want to get creative, you can add any of your favorite special effects to make the type more dimensional or textural.

This is the basic cast shadow. Now let's enhance the effect with a few more steps:

Step 1.

Start from scratch. Delete the contents of this image, or create a brand new image with the same dimensions and attributes as before.

Step 2.

Using the Type tool, create some new type in the document.

Step 3.

Choose **Copy** from the **Edit** menu.

Step 4.

While the type is still selected, either select a medium gray foreground color and then, choose **Fill** from the **Edit** menu. Or choose **Brightness/Contrast** from the **Adjust** submenu of the **Image** menu, and set the Brightness to 100%. As before, you want to create a medium gray selection that will become the cast shadow.

Step 5.

Choose **Skew** from the **Effects** submenu of the **Image** menu.

Step 6.

Drag one of the upper handles to the right to create a skewed selection. Click inside the selection to effect the change.

Step 7.

Choose the Gradient tool. Make sure the Gradient tool is set to a linear fill.

Step 8.

Set the foreground and background colors to white and black.

Step 9.

If the Brushes Palette is not visible, display it by choosing **Show Brushes** from the **Window** menu. Set the Opacity to 100% and the mode to Lighten.

Step 10.

Using the Gradient tool, drag from the top of the selection to the bottom.

See how the selection seems to fade into the distance.

Step 11.

Choose **None** from the **Select** menu to deselect the shadow selection, or use the keyboard shortcut Command-D.

Step 12.

Choose **Paste** from the **Edit** menu to paste the original type selection over the cast shadow.

As before, you can add some creativity by coloring and giving dimension to the selection by using your favorite bag of Photoshop tricks.

This is a pretty dramatic enhancement to the cast shadow effect, and it's simple to accomplish. Follow these steps to enhance it even further:

Step 1.

Create a new document using the same dimensions as before.

Step 2.

Using the Type tool, create some new type in the document.

Step 3.

Choose **Copy** from the **Edit** menu.

Step 4.

While the type is still selected, either select a medium gray foreground color and then, choose **Fill** from the **Edit** menu. Or choose **Brightness/Contrast** from the **Adjust** submenu of the **Image** menu, and set the Brightness to 100%. Either way, you want to create a medium gray selection that will become the cast shadow.

Step 5.

Choose **Skew** from the **Effects** submenu of the **Image** menu.

Step 6.

Drag one of the upper handles to the right to create a skewed selection. Click inside the selection to effect the change.

Step 7.

Using the Rectangular Marquee tool, select the entire top third of the shadow.

Step 8.

Choose **Feather** from the **Select** menu. Set the Feather radius to 12 pixels.

Step 9.

It might help to hide the edges of the selection. Choose **Hide Edges** from the **Select** menu (or press Command-H).

Step 10.

Choose **Blur More** from the **Blur** submenu of the **Filter** menu.

Step 11.

Repeat this filter by pressing Command-F a dozen or so more times until you get a nice indistinct cast shadow receding into the distance.

The reasoning behind making such small incremental changes in the blur is to make a more precise and gradual blur. If you used the Gaussian Blur command, it would happen all at once. This way, you have more control and a better result because repeating the Blur command also affects the previous blur effect.

Step 12.

Choose **None** from the **Select** menu (or press Command-D) to deselect the feathered shadow.

Step 13.

Choose **Paste** from the **Edit** menu to paste the clipboard selection over the shadow.

Step 14.

Move the copy into place by clicking on it and dragging it into position. You can also use the arrow cursor keys to nudge the new selection one pixel at a time for better control and precision.

There now: three simple ways to create a cast shadow, each more dramatic in its effect. You can add your own tricks, using extra channels and your favorite texture to add color, texture, and dimension to the type selection.

Creating Special Type Effects

In this section, you learn a few new techniques to add some special effects to your type treatments. You start with the basics and work your way up to more complex, but stunning, effects. These effects work well with solid colors or with textures applied. The beauty of these techniques is that they all employ simple tools and filters.

The more advanced effects require some close attention to the step-by-step functions and the order in which you take them.

Rounded Text

Creating rounded text is easy, but requires a few extra steps in the channel mode. Follow these steps:

Step 1.

Create a new document measuring 640 by 480 pixels in RGB Color mode, with a resolution of 72 pixels/inch.

Step 2.

Using the Type tool, create some text by clicking in the center of the work area and defining the font characteristics. Use your favorite typeface and make the text fairly large.

Step 3.

Click the foreground color swatch and choose a new foreground color for maximum effect.

Step 4.

Choose **Fill** from the **Edit** menu. Set the Opacity to 100% and fill your type selection with the foreground color.

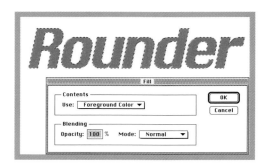

Step 5.

Choose **Show Channels** from the **Window** menu.

Step 6.

Click the top right corner of the Channels palette to display a pop-up menu. Choose **New Channel**.

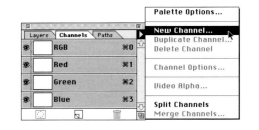

Step 7.

Give the new channel a name and click OK.

You will see the letterforms already selected from the RGB channel.

Step 8.

Use black as the foreground color and fill the selection. Remember, you can quickly choose black and white as the foreground and background colors by clicking the Default Colors icon in the lower left corner of the Tool palette.

This gives you a well-defined shape to reselect later.

Here's where the real fun begins. Next, create a new selection to turn into the highlighted side of the letters. Follow these steps:

Step 1.

Hold down the Command and Option keys. Press the down-arrow key three times and press the right-arrow key three times.

Holding down the Command and Option keys together enables you to move the selection marquee without moving the contents of the selection. Using the arrow keys moves the marquee one pixel at a time, which is crucial because you need to measure and control the distance that your selection moves.

Step 2.

Choose the Magic Wand tool. Hold down the Shift key and click anywhere in the background to select just the areas that occur between the actual image and the current selection area.

The Magic Wand tool should select the whole background in this example. Holding down the Shift key adds this selection to the current preexisting selection. So now, the selection surrounding and offset from the type is added to the background selection that you have just created, leaving the top left three pixels of the letter forms unselected.

Note: Notice how the interiors of the letters with closed loops (R, o, d, and e) are not selected now. To include them in the selection you can either hold down the Shift key and use the Magic Wand tool to continue selecting the interiors, or choose Similar from the Select menu. Either of these methods will include the interiors of these letters with the selection.

Next, you want to add subtle soft highlights to the upper and left edges of the type in the RGB channel, but everything except those areas is selected. Let's change that:

Step 1.

Choose **Inverse** from the **Select** menu to invert the selected areas.

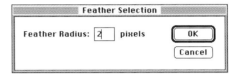

Now to add a bit of highlight to the characters.

Step 2.

Return to the RGB channel by clicking on its name in the Channels palette, or press Command-0.

You could choose **Fill** from the **Edit** menu and add the foreground color as a shaded highlight. But let's use a more polished and realistic approach.

Step 3.

Choose **Feather** from the **Select** menu. Set the Feather radius to a conservative 2 pixels.

Now, any effect you apply to the selection is blended into the background subtly across a radius of two pixels.

Step 4.

Click the Switch Colors icon next to the color swatches in the Tool palette to set the foreground color to white.

Step 5.

Choose **Hide Edges** from the **Select** menu (or press Command-H) to hide the selection marquee to get a clearer picture of the changes you're making.

Step 6.

Choose **Fill** from the **Edit** menu. Set the Opacity to 100%.

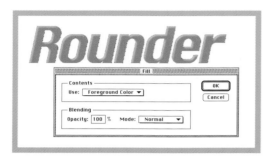

If this isn't light enough for your tastes, play with the Opacity setting until you achieve the contrast you want. The concept behind this technique is that you get to finesse the shading in a couple of steps rather than strong-arming it in one big step.

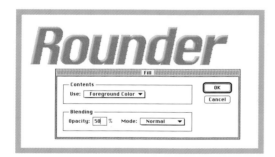

Now that you have applied a nice, soft, highlighted edge to the type, let's add an opposite shadow with just as much softness to it:

Step 1.

Go to the extra channel by clicking once on its name in the Channels palette.

Step 2.

Using the Magic Wand tool, click one of the letters to select the text.

Step 3.

Choose **Similar** from the **Select** menu. (Alternatively, you could also choose to select each letter individually using the Magic Wand tool while you hold down the Shift key.)

Step 4.

Hold down the Option and Command keys. Press the up-arrow key three times and press the left-arrow key three times.

Step 5.

Hold down the Shift key and use the Magic Wand tool to click the white background and add the background to the selection.

Step 6.

Choose **Similar** from the **Select** menu to make sure that you're including the interiors of the loop letters.

Choose **Inverse** from the **Select** menu to invert the selected areas.

Step 7.

Return to the RGB channel.

Step 8.

Choose **Feather** from the **Select** menu. Set the Feather radius to 2 pixels.

Time to add the feathered shadow side of the letters.

Step 1.

Switch the foreground color to black by clicking the Switch Colors icon in the tool palette.

Step 2.

Choose **Fill** from the **Edit** menu. Set the Opacity to 30%. You can reapply this fill as many times as you want to get the effect you are looking for. Choose **Hide Edges** from the **Select** menu to get a better view of the effect of the filter.

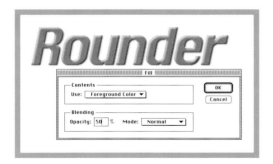

As you apply successive shades of black to these shadowed areas, you may notice that the shadow is bleeding into the background. You might want to leave this in for effect, but in this exercise, you take it out now to clean up the outside of the image. Follow these steps:

Step 1.

Go to the extra channel by clicking once on its name in the Channels palette.

Step 2.

Using the Magic Wand tool, click one of the letters to select the text. Choose **Similar** from the **Select** menu to choose all the letters. (or press Command-0)

Step 3.

Return to the RGB composite channel.

Step 4.

Choose **Inverse** from the **Select** menu to select the entire background.

Select	Window
All	⌘A
None	⌘D
Inverse	
Float	⌘J
Color Range...	
Feather...	
Modify	▶
Matting	▶
Grow	⌘G
Similar	
Hide Edges	⌘H
Load Selection...	
Save Selection...	

Step 5.

Make sure that the background color is set to white, and then press the Delete key to remove everything in the selection. This effectively cleans up everything in the background of the image, leaving a clean edge to the rounded type.

Alternatively, you could choose Fill from the Edit menu to fill the selection with another color or pattern of your choice.

Step 6.

Choose **Inverse** from the **Select** menu again. This reselects the type outline.

Note: Remember, to get a clearer picture of what you're doing, you can hide the selection marquee before applying any filter or effect. Just choose **Hide Edges** from the **Select** menu.

Your image is almost complete. It looks pretty clean, although the edges are rather sharp and jagged. Let's dress it up a little more with an outline. Follow these steps:

Step 1.

Click once on the foreground color swatch and choose a contrasting foreground color. How about a nice blue?

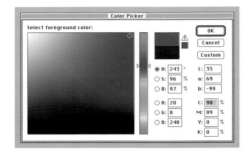

Step 2.

While the type is still selected, choose **Stoke** from the **Edit** menu to apply an outline or border to the selection.

Step 3.

Make the stroke two pixels surrounding the center of the selection marquee.

Looks great. And what a powerful technique to use in future renderings! Remember, you can create art like this at whatever resolution you want. The examples presented are at 72 dpi (the normal screen resolution of the computer monitor). You can create these same effects at much higher resolutions for your own high-quality print work.

You can always add your own special touch to any illustration using any of the other techniques that you have already learned, for example, a fuzzy drop shadow or some airbrushed glings.

This same effect is as easily applied to a basic shape as type and letter forms. This effect makes for dramatic backgrounds, textures, and buttons for any multimedia project.

Neon Text

Another great effect that looks great and only takes a few steps to accomplish is neon text. You can use this technique almost anywhere, and even create a custom glowing effect over existing documents. Follow these steps:

Step 1.

Create a new document measuring 640 by 480 pixels in RGB Color mode, with a resolution of 72 pixels/inch.

Step 2.

Choose **Show Channels** from the **Window** menu.

Step 3.

Click the top right corner of the Channels palette to display a pop-up menu. Choose New Channel.

Step 4.

Name the new channel anything you want and click OK.

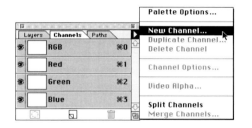

Step 5.

In this new channel, create a large type object using the Type tool and choosing a fairly thin sans-serif type style. The reason for creating the type in the extra channel is that you will be selecting and reselecting the type shapes to apply different filters and effects and you will need a clean, sharp-edged version to select in some steps.

The type selection is active in the RGB channel, where you will apply all the filters and effects.

Step 6.

Return to the RGB channel, where you will see the selection is still active.

Step 7.

Make sure the foreground and background colors are currently black and white.

Step 8.

Choose **Feather** from the **Select** menu. Set the Feather Radius to 4 pixels.

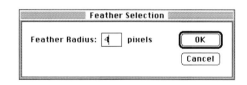

Step 9.

Choose **Stroke** from the **Edit** menu. Set the stroke width to 3 pixels and select the Center radio button.

Now that was easy! Let's adjust the brightness and contrast a bit to give the creation a more solid look, and let's add some color.

Step 1.

Choose **Brightness/Contrast** from the **Adjust** submenu of the **Image** menu. Increase the level of contrast by entering a value of 50 or by moving the Contrast slider to the right.

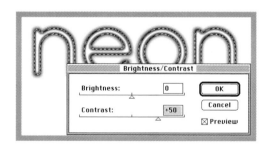

Step 2.

Choose **Hue/Saturation** from the **Adjust** submenu of the **Image** menu. Click the Preview and Colorize check boxes and move the Hue slider around to get your favorite neon color.

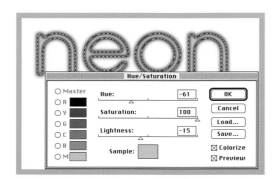

Step 3.

Choose **Inverse** from the **Select** menu.

Step 4.

Choose **Invert** from the **Map** submenu of the **Image** menu to place the neon type onto a dark background.

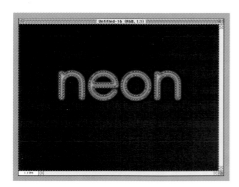

You may notice that the image looks slightly artificial, with a pale gray glow around a wonderfully colorful neon tube. Let's add some color to the background:

Step 1.

Using the Eyedropper tool, click one of the most colorful pixel in the neon text.

Step 2.

Choose **Fill** from the **Edit** menu. Set the Opacity to 100% and the mode to Color.

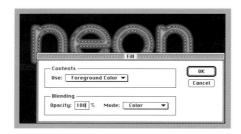

This fills all the lighter areas with the selected foreground color.

Step 3.

Choose **Inverse** from the **Select** menu to reselect the neon type.

Step 4.

Choose **Brightness/Contrast** from the **Adjust** submenu of the **Image** menu. Slide the Contrast slider to the right until you get a nicely contrasted color effect in the selection area.

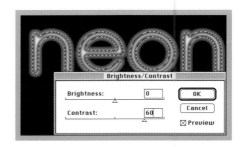

Step 5.

You can clean up the selection a little more by reselecting a clean-edged version of the type in the extra channel (without feathering the selection) and applying a black stroke around the type shapes.

Step 6.

Select the type in the extra channel by clicking one of he letters and choosing **Similar** from the **Select** menu. Return to the RGB channel.

Step 7.

Make sure the foreground color is set to black. Choose **Stroke** from the **Edit** menu. Set the line weight to an appropriate thickness and click OK.

Carved Stone Letters

Here's a technique that you can use to carve anything into stone. You will be able to create your own thousand-year-old hieroglyphics with natural-looking rough-hewn weathered edges, classic bas-relief letter forms, home-made chiseled-into-polished stone letters and signs—all with a few simple steps in Photoshop.

You need some nice rocky texture into which you will carve the letter forms. You can open one of the fine granite or sandstone textures you created earlier in the book, or you can create something new. You create a new channel to place the selectable type and then you move back and forth between the two channels to apply the effects.

It's actually a fairly simple process. The trick is in knowing what order to apply the filters. Let's start by creating a worn and weathered piece of history carved into sandstone.

Follow these steps:

Step 1.

Either open an existing texture and duplicate it, or start fresh with a new document.

Step 2.

Choose **Show Channels** from the **Window** menu.

Step 3.

Click the top right corner of the Channels palette to display a pop-up menu. Choose New Channel.

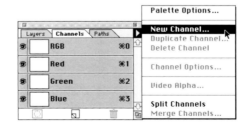

Step 4.

Name the new channel anything you want and click OK.

Step 5.

In this channel, create a new type object using the Type tool. Make it fairly large in the window.

Just for extra effect, let's add a little roughness to the shape of the letters.

Step 1.

While the letter forms are still selected, Choose **Feather** from the **Select** menu Set the Feather Radius to 12 pixels.

Step 2.

To apply a mild ripple effect, choose **Ripple** from the **Distort** submenu of the **Filter** menu. Set the amount to 100 and click the large radio button.

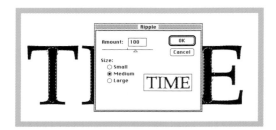

By feathering the selection first, you're making a very graduated transition across the selection. And, by applying a very mild ripple to the selection, you're starting to make them look almost hand-carved.

Now to continue the process:

Step 1.

Deselect everything.

Step 2.

Using the Magic Wand tool, click one of the letters to select the text.

Step 3.

Choose **Similar** from the **Select** menu.

Step 4.

Return to the RGB channel.

Step 5.

Choose **Feather** from the **Select** menu. Set the Feather radius to 2 pixels.

Step 6.

Choose **Brightness/Contrast** from the **Adjust** submenu of the **Image** menu and darken the selection a bit.

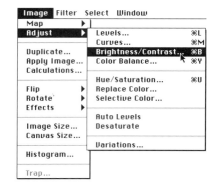

This will be the darker shadowed area of the hand-carved effect.

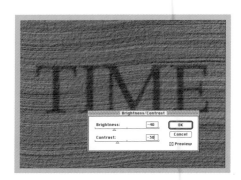

Step 7.

You might try using the keyboard shortcut Command-H to hide the selection marquee, giving yourself a better view of the change.

This is a good start to the effect, but to really give it more definition and dimension, you need to add a highlighted edge to one side:

Step 1.

Go back to the extra channel

Step 2.

Using the Magic Wand tool, click one of the letters to reselect the text.

Step 3.

Choose **Similar** from the **Select** menu.

Step 4.

Hold down the Option and Command keys. Press the left-arrow key twice and press the up-arrow key twice. This moves only the selection (not its contents) up and to the left two pixels.

Step 5.

Hold down the Shift key while you use the Magic Wand tool to click once in the background. This selects all the white background pixels, adding them to the selection. Choose **Similar** from the **Select** menu to select the interiors of letters with closed loops.

Step 6.

Of course, your objective is to select just the edge pixels that are now left out of the selection, so choose **Inverse** from the **Select** menu.

Step 7.

Return to the RGB channel. The selection is still active.

Step 8.

Choose **Feather** from the **Select** menu. Set the Feather Radius to 1 pixel (or 2, depending on how indistinct you want the effect to be).

Step 9.

Choose **Brightness/Contrast** from the **Adjust** submenu of the **Image** menu and set the brightness to about 40 to lighten up the selected area.

See how this effect adds some depth and life to the effect? Now let's enhance the effect by adding just a hint of shadow accent to the interior of the carved area:

Step 1.

Go back to the extra channel.

Step 2.

Using the Magic Wand tool, select the harder edged type.

Step 3.

Choose **Similar** from the **Select** menu.

Step 4.

Hold down the Option and Command keys. Press the down-arrow key two times and press the right-arrow key two times to move the selection down and to the right by two pixels.

Step 5.

Hold down the Shift key and use the Magic Wand tool to select all the background pixels.

Step 6.

Choose **Inverse** from the **Select** menu to select only the upper left two pixels of the type shapes.

Step 7.

Return to the RGB channel.

Step 8.

Choose **Feather** from the **Select** menu. Set the Feather radius to 1 pixel because you want this final application to be fairly subtle.

Step 9.

Choose **Brightness/Contrast** from the **Adjust** submenu of the **Image** menu. Reduce the brightness of the selection a bit, making the interior of the feathered selection just a bit darker.

As you can see, the magic lies in the application of feathered and offset highlight and shadow areas.

You can create a variation of the effect, making the highlights and shadows similar, but with a smooth interior texture. This effect works great in either direction, depending on the light source, making it either chiseled out of stone or a simple bas-relief effect.

Let's try a little different effect to create type that is more sharply defined and stamped into the texture in few different ways. Follow these steps:

Step 1.

Create a new document measuring 640 by 480 pixels in RGB Color mode, with a resolution of 72 pixels/inch.

Step 2.

Choose **Add Noise** from the **Noise** submenu of the **Filter** menu. Set the Noise value to 999 and the distribution to Gaussian to create a quick and easy sandstone texture.

Step 3.

Choose **Emboss** from the **Stylize** submenu of the **Filter** menu. Set the angle to 135°, the height to 1 pixel, and the amount to 100%.

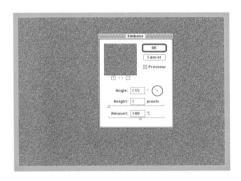

Step 4.

Choose **Hue/Saturation** from the **Adjust** submenu of the **Image** menu. Click both the Colorize and Preview check boxes. Color the background by moving the sliders around until you get a sandy texture.

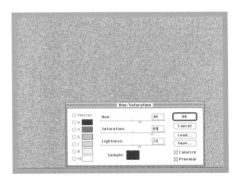

That was easy enough. If you're using a macro key utility such as Tempo or QuicKeys, you can assign a simple function key equivalent to any or all of these operations to automate this process.

Now to create your text:

Step 1.

Choose **Show Channels** from the **Window** menu.

Step 2.

Click the top right corner of the Channels palette to display a pop-up menu. Choose New Channel.

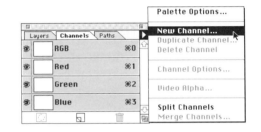

Step 3.

Give the new channel a name, and click OK.

Step 4.

In the new channel, create some type.

You will select and reselect this type to create the new effect. For this exercise, use the Chicago typeface because it's a native Macintosh typeface. Typically, this technique works best with a sans-serif typeface, the bolder the better.

Step 5.

Return to the RGB channel. The outline of the type in the extra channel is still visible.

Step 6.

Choose **Copy** from the **Edit** menu. You will use this copy of the selection later to paste over some gradient effects applied to the textured background.

Time to create some indented shadow areas:

Step 1.

Return to the extra channel by clicking its name in the Channels palette. The type should still be selected. (If not, use the Magic Wand tool and the Similar command from the Select menu to reselect all the letterforms.)

Step 2.

Hold down the Command and Option keys. Press the down-arrow key three times and press the right-arrow key three times to move the selection marquee down and to the right 3 pixels.

Step 3.

Hold down the Shift key and use the Magic Wand tool to click in the background. This adds the background white pixels to the selection.

If the type has occluded areas (like the interior of the lowercase 'e'), choose **Similar** from the **Select** menu to include them in the selection.

Step 4.

Choose **Inverse** from the **Select** menu to select just the upper left edges of the type shapes.

Step 5.

Return to the RGB channel.

Step 6.

Choose **Feather** from the **Select** menu. Set the Feather radius to 4 pixels.

Step 7.

Choose **Brightness/Contrast** from the **Adjust** submenu of the **Image** menu. Increase the brightness of the selection.

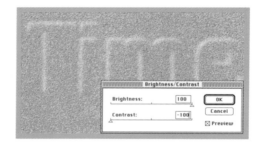

By feathering the selection, you create a more mellow transition between the background texture and the selected pixels. This is a good start to an easy effect.

Let's use the same technique in the opposite direction to select just the bottom right pixels of the type:

Step 1.

Return to the extra channel.

Step 2.

Use the Magic Wand tool to select one of the letters.

Step 3.

Choose **Similar** from the **Select** menu.

Step 4.

Hold down the Option and Command keys. Press the up-arrow key three times and press the left-arrow key three times.

Step 5.

Hold down the Shift key and use the Magic Wand tool to select the background.

Step 6.

Choose **Similar** from the **Select** menu to include the interiors of any looped letters.

Step 7.

Choose **Inverse** from the **Select** menu. You have the selection!

Step 8.

Return to the RGB channel.

Step 9.

Choose **Feather** from the **Select** menu. Leave the Feather radius at 4 pixels.

Step 10.

Choose **Brightness/Contrast** from the **Adjust** submenu of the **Image** menu. Make the new selection darker by reducing the brightness and increasing the contrast as much as possible.

Not a bad effect so far. But, of course, you can enhance it still further.

Step 11.

Since the selected (and unaltered) type is still on the clipboard, choose **Paste** from the **Edit** menu and paste it over the selection.

Step 12.

Move it into position using the mouse or the arrow cursor keys.

There it is. A nice subtle effect that can be enhanced in a number of ways. You can increase the depth of the image by creating a larger feather radius when you create the highlighted and shadowed areas.

You can also add an outline or color the selection.

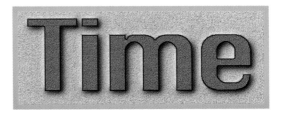

Carved Rounded Sandstone Text

How about combining two techniques to create something even more dramatic? In this section, you combine the dimensional type technique and the textural type technique to simulate a carved, rounded sandstone effect. Follow these steps:

Step 1.

Open an existing texture document or create a new rough texture, using your favorite tried-and-true texture creation techniques.

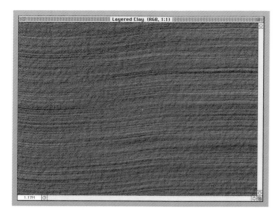

Step 2.

Choose **Duplicate** from the **Calculate** submenu of the **Image** menu to create a duplicate image into which you can paste new work later.

Step 3.

Create a new channel and place some large sans-serif type in it. You'll need to select this type again later.

Step 8.

Return to the RGB channel.

Step 9.

Choose **Feather** from the **Select** menu. Set the Feather radius to 6 pixels to achieve a rounded effect. (You can set the Feather radius to 3 pixels for a less rounded effect.)

Step 10.

Choose **Brightness/Contrast** from the **Adjust** submenu of the **Image** menu. Adjust the brightness and contrast to make the selection darker.

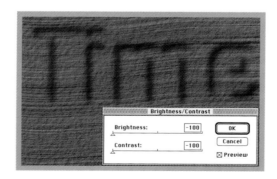

Step 11.

Return to the extra channel.

Step 12.

Use the Magic Wand tool and click one of the letters choose **Similar** from the **Select** menu to reselect all of the type shapes.

Step 13.

Hold down the Command and Option keys. Press the up-arrow key and the left-arrow key to select just the bottom right pixels.

Step 14.

Use the Magic Wand tool and the Similar and Inverse commands under the Select menu to select just the lower right edges of the type selection.

Step 15.

Return to the RGB channel.

Step 16.

Choose **Feather** from the **Select** menu. Leave the feather radius at whatever the last setting was. You want this lighter area to equally offset the darker area you just created.

Step 17.

Choose **Brightness/Contrast** from the **Adjust** submenu of the **Image** menu. This time, make the selection brighter instead of darker.

This effect is pretty dramatic in its own right. You may want to save this document as an example of a nice "mound-o-type" effect to use later.

Let's continue with the exercise. Follow these steps:

Step 1.

Return to the extra channel.

Step 2.

Using the Magic Wand tool, click one of the letters.

Step 3.

Choose **Similar** from the **Select** menu to select all the type shapes.

Step 4.

Go back to the RGB channel.

Step 5.

Choose **Copy** from the **Edit** menu.

Step 6.

Open or activate the plain texture document and paste this selection into it.

Not a bad effect. If you require a little more definition to the type sample, choose **Stroke** from the **Edit** menu and place a simple stroke around the type.

You can also combine the same effect in different layers and opposite directions to enhance the effect even further.

Chapter 8

Artist's Gallery

The artist's gallery is a place for you to get new ideas on how to use Photoshop to your best advantage. Most of the artists depicted use Photoshop in conjunction with other software packages, specialized hardware, and photographic images. However, the techniques you've learned in the past chapters are the basics of what many of them do every day.

   All of the images here are owned by the individual artist who created them. Please respect the work that went into making them by not using them in your own work without their permission. Details on how to reach each of the artists has been included in the descriptions of the individual work.

Greg Vander Houwen

Greg Vander Houwen is a professional graphic artist and Photoshop instructor in Issaquah, Washington. Greg was kind enough to not only share some of his work for this book, but also to give some insights into how he created his images.

Paragon of Distraction

The ring was then placed into the Photoshop image and its reflection was painted into the ripples of the water. The border was created using the selection tools of Photoshop and then filled using differing amounts of opacity.

The first image, Paragon of Distraction, was created with Adobe Photoshop and Strata Vision 3d. The hardware used to create the images included:

- a Mac SE30 and a Mac IIx,
- a Nikon LS-3500 slide scanner,
- a Hewlett-Packard ScanJet Plus,
- a Wacom tablet,
- a LVT film recorder, and
- a Minolta Maxxum 35mm SLR.

Techniques

The image was created from three primary elements—the sky/water, the arm, and the ring. The sky was photographed in eastern Washington. It was flipped, distorted, and filtered to become the water element. The "water" was then placed and painted into position below the sky. The hand was placed into the composite image and its reflection was painted into the ripples.

The ring was created by rendering a three-dimensional wire frame that had a gold metal texture attached. The object was placed into a Strata Vision 3d "room" that had the sky and mater images attached to the walls. The ring reflected the "walls" of the room and picked up the look of polished metal.

Cloud Burst

The second image, Cloud Burst, was created using Adobe Photoshop, Adobe Illustrator, and Fractal Design Painter. You can "test drive" Fractal Design Painter with the demo enclosed on the accompanying CD-ROM in the back of the book. The hardware used to create this image included:

- a Mac SE30 and a Quadra 950,
- a Nikon slide scanner and an Isomet drum scanner,
- a Wacom 6 by 9 tablet
- a LVT film recorder.

Techniques

This image was created from four elements—the clouds, waterfall, desert, and stars. It started as a background composite of the desert and sky. Selection masks were extracted from the composite and filtration was applied through them. The fog was painted in to appear as though it had settled into the small valleys.

In a separate document, the waterfall was separated from its background and then opened in Fractal Design Painter to have a paper texture applied. The waterfall was then composited into the desert/sky image through a semi-transparent mask.

The stars were created in Illustrator where they were distorted and scaled for placement in the Photoshop image. Finally, the image frame was created using a combination of fills and map inversions.

Greg Vender Houwen can be reached at Interact, PO Box 498, Issaquah, Washington 98027. Paragon of Distraction is copyright 1990 and Cloudburst is copyright 1994 by Greg Vander Houwen. All rights are reserved by the artist.

Dorothy Simpson Krause

Dorothy Simpson Krause is a Professor of Computer Graphics in the Department of Design for the Massachusetts College of Art. Dorothy's images are also contained on the accompanying CD-ROM in the back of the book.

Anatomy Lesson

Anatomy Lesson was created on a Mac Quadra 700 using Adobe Photoshop from several source images:

- A Lady With a Squirrel and a Starling by Holbein (1526-1528),
- watch by Breuget for Marie Antoinette, and
- Canon of Medicine by the Persian ibn Sina or Avicenna (980-1037)

Wasteland

Wasteland was created from two images—one of a woman and one of an abandoned barren landscape. It was created on a Mac Quadra 700 using Adobe Photoshop.

Anatomy Lesson and Wasteland are both copyright 1993 by Dorothy Simpson Krause. All rights are reserved by the artist. You can reach Dorothy through Mary Lou Bock, Director, The Williams Gallery, 8 Chambers Street, Princeton, New Jersey 08542.

Bill Niffenegger

Bill Niffenegger is a painter, sculptor, and illustrator based in Cloudcroft, New Mexico. In addition to his fine arts activities, he currently produces complex computer imaging illustrations for many major clients. All of Bill's images are digitally painted using a combination of Adobe Photoshop, Fractal Design Painter, Infini-D, Stratavision, and Kai's Power Tools filters as well as other plug-in filters.

Harlequin

Harlequin is an experiment in digital effects. Each sphere illustrates a complex "juggling" of color overlay effects. The harlequin figure has been entirely hand-painted within the computer.

Opulent Fauna

Opulent Fauna is a computer-generated painting that utilizes small samplings of nature photography. These elements are cloned, distorted, and composited with hand-painted portions to produce a quite striking creature. This image was created for presentation in a Tokyo exhibition.

Harlequin and Opulent Fauna are both copyright 1993 by Bill Niffenegger. All rights are reserved by the artist. You can reach Bill at Niffenegger Studios, The Green Tree Lodge, 107 Grand Avenue, Cloudcroft, NM 88317. Bill can also be reached on the Internet at AFCBILL@AOL.COM.

Ian Gilman

Ian Gilman is a computer artist and programmer who resides in Winslow, Washington. Ian allowed us to place some of his work that came entirely from Photoshop's filters—no additional materials were required to create either of his entries. Both works are included on the CD-ROM in the back of the book.

Blooming Marbled

Blooming Marbled is a stylized reproduction of marbled paper. It can be used as a texture for any number of objects, backgrounds, or foregrounds. The somewhat unique feature of this reproduction is that it will tile seamlessly.

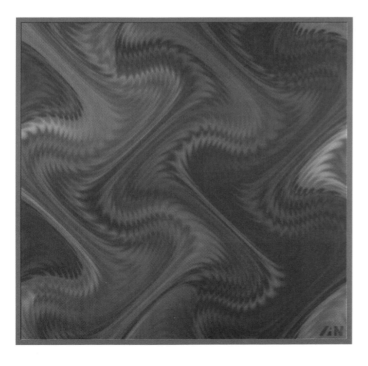

Carnal Jewel

Carnal Jewel is the result of many channel operations. The diamond shape was created by a simple rotation and the halo is a number of motion blurs calculated together. There are also some ripple and wave effects in the piece creating a virtual puzzle of how the artist created the work.

Both the images were created with Photoshop version 2.0 on a Mac IIfx without any additional filters, software packages, or special hardware.

Blooming Marbled and Carnal Jewel are both copyright 1993 by Ian Gilman. All rights are reserved by the artist. Ian Gilman can be reached by writing to 712 Cherry Avenue NE, Winslow, Washington 98110.

Dick Hanna

Dick Hanna is a professional artist residing in Denver, Colorado. Dick's work can also be found on the CD-ROM in the back of the book.

EarthRise

The original image is courtesy of the Denver Museum of Natural History/Gate Planetarium. The type for the word "one" was set and modified in Adobe Illustrator, then pasted in the document in a new channel. Masks were created using duplicate, offset, and subtract in the calculate commands and the highlights and shadows were created by adjusting output levels in the newly created masks.

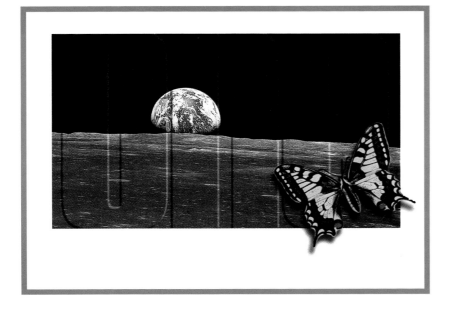

WineGlass

WineGlass contains an original photograph by Sims Photographics and demonstrates several techniques. The background shape and ragged edges were painted on canvas, scanned, and used as a mask to past the wineglass image into. The stain was created by dipping a wineglass in wine and placing it on an illustration board. This stain was then scanned and composited into the image using the paste command and composite controls set to multiply. The skyline was then pasted into the wineglss and a sheen was added over the image with the airbrush tool.

Dick Hanna can be reached at Studio One, 517 E. Fourth Avenue, Denver, CO 80203. EarthRise and WineGlass are both copyright 1993 and all rights are reserved by the artist.

Xaos Tools Artist in Residence Series

Xaos Tools shipped the first of their Artist in Residence series, Fresco, in May of 1994. They have graciously allowed us to reproduce Circles, an image created by George Larson from that series. Fresco is the first of CD-ROM products available from Xaos Tools Incorporated containing royalty-free images from fine artists. George Lawson is a San Francisco-based minimalist painter who created the 80 images contained on the CD-ROM.

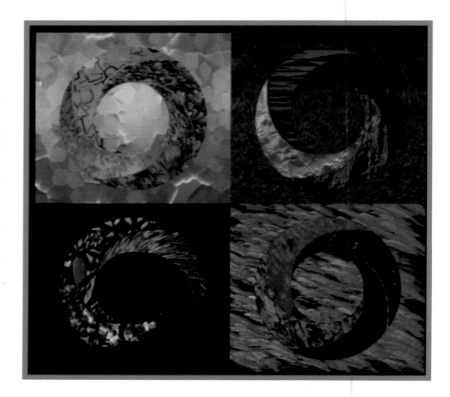

Circles

All of the images in Fresco were created using proprietary artificial intelligence technology developed by Xaos Tools co-founder and principal scientist, Michael Tolson. Circles is one of the images contained on the Fresco CD-ROM and comes in three resolutions:

- 24-bit, 72 dots per inch for placement and low-resolution output,

- 8-bit, 640X480 pixels for multimedia applications, and

- 24-bit, 300 dots per inch for high-resolution output.

Xaos Tools, Incorporated is an independent company and can be reached at 600 Townsend Street, Suite 270 East, San Francisco, California 94130. Circles is available as part of Fresco, a set of royalty-free images from Xaos Tools, Inc.

About the CD

A few years ago, this book would have been packaged with a disk in the back with perhaps a filter or two and a couple of sample images for you to play with. There would have been hundreds of images to choose from to include on the disk, there just wouldn't be enough space on the disk for them.

Now, with CD-ROM players becoming more popular (and the making of CD-ROMs becoming cheaper), it becomes not a decision of what to include, but rather a decision of how to organize all the information available. We've tried to organize the hundreds of files enclosed in a meaningful manner, but everyone organizes things a little differently. Therefore, we'll take a little time here to explain where exactly everything is.

The CD-ROM has been organized into five separate folders. They are:

- Artist Gallery,
- Filters,
- Fractal Design Painter, and
- Miles of Tiles.

Some of these folders have folders of their own so each of the main folders are detailed below. In general, all of the material on the CD-ROM was generated with Photoshop Versions 2.5 and 2.5.1 in mind. Version 3.0 wasn't quite on the shelves when this book was created and it was decided that, for compatibility reasons, all the images and filters should be useable in Version 2.5 as well as 3.0

Artist Gallery

The Artist Gallery folder contains the work of some of the artists you met in Chapter 8. Please remember that that each image is copyrighted by the individual artist and should not be used without their express permission. The images have been included here so that you can view their work directly in Photoshop and see how the channels and filters have been used first-hand. For more information on each individual artist, please refer to Chapter 8.

Filters

There are two folders inside this folder—each from a different company. KPT Filters contains a set of filters from Kai's Power Tools version 2.0 and a demo version of BRYCE New Worlds Explorer. For specific instructions on how to use the filters found in the KPT Filters folder, please see the Read Me! file inside the folder. Alien Skin Software contains another filter from a different company.

B.R.Y.C.E contains a demo version of New Worlds Explorer, a stand-alone Macintosh application that designs natural and supernatural landscapes. This is the only part of the CD-ROM that requires software other than Photoshop to preview. You must have the QuickTime Extension installed to view the images. To install BRYCE, open the **BRYCE DISK 1** folder and double click on **BRYCE Teaser Install**. The installation program will ask for the last portion of BRYCE. The last segment can be found in the BRYCE DISK 4 folder.

As mentioned above, the other folder in the Filters folder is called Alien Skin Software. Alien Skin Software is the maker of The Black Box, another set of plug-in filters for Photoshop. The filter inside the Alien Skin Software folder is a Drop Shadow filter and is contained in a self-extracting archive. Double click on **Drop Shadow 1.1e.sea** and tell your computer where you would like the files to be decompressed. Please read the Read Me file from the archive for further information on the filter. The Alien Skin Software folder also contains two sample images in JPEG format that demonstrate the Drop Shadow filter and other filters from The Black Box.

Fractal Design Painter

There are no additional folders inside this folder. What is in the folder is a demo of Fractal Design Painter Version 2.0. You'll be able to try out all the features of Fractal Design Painter and see how it will fit in with your everyday life if you should decide to buy it. At the very least, try running the two demos, **Fire** and **splat**, that come with the demo. You'll get a quick look at the power and flexibility of this exciting design tool. You'll also get a chance to play with an exciting application that could help you in your work.

Images

Now we start getting to the stuff you can actually use with no strings attached. Images contains four folders, Free Planets, Fresco, Images, and It's texturific. Each of these images can go right into your bag of tricks without the trouble of creating them by hand. I've inserted a sample file from each folder to help you find things a little easier.

Free Planets

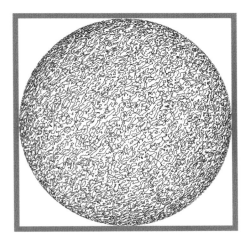

We created some planets earlier in the book. Here are some prefabricated worlds you can use in your work. All of the worlds have the planet itself saved in an extra channel to make selecting them out of their backgrounds easier.

Fresco

Another set of images from the people at HSC Software, the makers of Kai's Power Tools. Fresco is a set of 80 royalty-free textural images created by George Lawson using artificial intelligence created by Xaos Tools.

Images

You might recognize this image as the one from the cover of this book. With a few slight alterations, it was used as the background for the cover art. Images are a few backgrounds you might find useful as starting points for your own work or even for ideas of what to create next.

It's Texturific

We created a lot of these in learning the techniques throughout the book. However, here are a few images to create a texture library of your own that you can refer to again and again.

Metals

Streaks

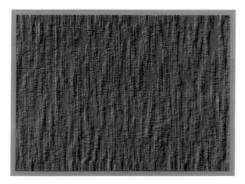

Strange Brew

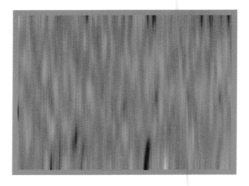

Weaves

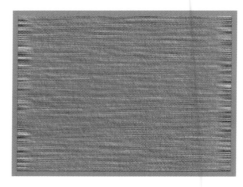

Stuccos

Rocks

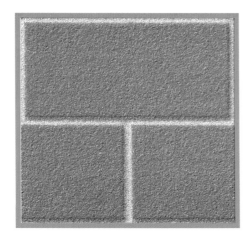

Woods

Miles of Tiles

The last folder is titled Miles of Tiles. It contains eight folders of individual tiled textures. These individual folders are titled:

Bathroom Tiles,

Clay Tiles,

CinderBlocks,

Aluminum,

Generic Square Tiles,

Bricks,

Wild Tiles, and

Wood Tiles.

All of these tiled textures make fantastic backgrounds and textures for nearly anything. Hopefully you'll find something to your liking here (my personal favorites are in Wild Tiles). In any case, there's well over 100 megabytes of images, filters, and software for you to try out here on the CD-ROM. It, by itself, is worth much more than the price of this book.

Enjoy your new techniques, your new filters, your new image library, and your demo of Fractal Design Painter!